Manningtree and Mistley

Manningtree was a tightly knit town when this engraving, from a drawing by W. Bartlett, was published in 1832. One could still see a similar view from the heights of Lawford until about 1970, after which rapid development obscured the distant scene.

MANNINGTREE AND MISTLEY

The people, the trades and industries past and present.

David Cleveland

Revised, corrected and updated edition
2012

This book was originally published by
Malthouse Press
Holbrook
Suffolk
2007

This revised, corrected and updated version published by
David Cleveland
Manningtree
Essex

ISBN 978-0-9558271-5-0

British Library Cataloguing-in-Publication Data
A catalogue record for this book is available from the British Library.

Designed by Ken Rickwood

Printed in Great Britain by
Lavenham Press Ltd.

Contents

Mistley Quay with Richard Rigby's church with the twin towers in the middle distance.
This engraving was published by George Vertue in 1831.

Preface

This is a new and updated (and corrected) version of the book that Malthouse Press published in 2007, in which I wrote in the Preface: "I have lived in Manningtree since 1969, and have slowly absorbed information about the town, neighbouring Mistley, the River Stour, and aspects of the area's history. I have always been interested in the past and how it connects with the present, and have wanted to know how things were done in former times.

Many people have given or lent photographs, and I have taken some myself over the years. Books, pamphlets, and people's reminiscences have come my way. My wife, who worked in Manningtree Library, knows many local people and has picked up a great deal of the history and life of the area over the years.

So, as an amateur, and an incomer to the area, I have tried to put together all these pieces of information into this book, which takes a gentle look at Manningtree and Mistley. Originally I thought of a picture book, then I added 'fragments of history', and then a walk around the town. As you can see the project grew and grew. I have tried, though, to restrict it to Manningtree and Mistley. I have not included much about Lawford as Ivan Sage produced the excellent book *'Lawford Life'* in 2002. Other books that give a huge amount of information and history about Manningtree and Mistley are listed in the bibliography at the end of this book.

As these books have so much in them, I have avoided as much as possible duplicating information and copying photographs already published. I leave the reader to find these books and enjoy them.

I am not an historian, just someone interested in the place I live. Any mistakes or incorrect information I apologise for, but would like to hear from the reader so I can adjust this for the future. Many people have helped me with information, pictures, answers to questions, pointed me in certain directions, and generally encouraged me. They are listed below, but my biggest thanks must go to Bob Malster, who edited the book, corrected many mistakes, added vital information, and wrote linking sections to make the book sensible and readable.

I wish to thank the following: Charles Bolton, Richard Brooks, Ethel Cook, Maryan Fidler, Jack Field, David Foster, Peter Gant, Joan Godsave, Norman Harbach, Bob Horlock, David Kindred, Tony Lansdown, Lesley Pallett, Doreen Parsons, Ann Patterson, Jim Pittock, Ian Rose, Katherine Rose, Bill Rose, Cora Townes, Dora Whent, and Robin Wilshaw".

For this revised and corrected edition I would like to thank: John Adams, Andy Birch, Jane Blanchflower, Barbara Bolton, Linda Borg, Andrew Brinkley, Pamela Browne, Gill Carey, Jenine Collier, Dean Coulson, Philip Cunningham, Neil Jones, Allan 'Dusty' Miller, David Shearmur, Ben Simmons, Rosemary Smith, Anita Stone, Val Taylor, Carole Versey, Ann Ward, David Webb, John Wood, Manningtree Museum and Local History Group, and Ken Rickwood for his usual excellent design and layout, as well as seeing to the maps.

David Cleveland
2012

Above: Manningtree High Street in 2011.   *Below:* Mistley High Street in 2011.

Joseph Glass's book of Manningtree published in 1855.

And so through woods, in some auspicious hour,
Came to the banks of this our River Stour.
To build their huts they cleared away the trees;
And thus the village rose by small degrees;
And as the place advanced, we must allow,
'Twas strange that they should call it Schidingeou.

Introduction

Joseph Glass, the author of 'Reminiscences of Manningtree and its Vicinity', which was published in 1855, was not really a native of Manningtree, having been born in Colchester in 1792, but he spent his early life in Manningtree and obviously absorbed all that was going on around him in his teenage years. Half a century later he set down, mainly in verse, his memories of that 'pleasant market town, as broad as long, and is of some renown'.

It was while in Manningtree that he became a teetotaller, but it wasn't long before he moved on, first to Bristol and then to London. Having reached London he set up a chimney-sweeping and building business, inventing a mechanical method of sweeping chimneys at a time when people were campaigning for the abolition of climbing boys. His device, which included an efficient means of connecting the flexible rods needed to negotiate bends in a chimney, became widely used after 1829, when Sir Robert Peel authorised its use in government offices. Glass received a medal for his invention, and a prize of £200.

Joseph Glass was in his sixties when he wrote his *'Reminiscences of Manningtree and its Vicinity'*, which was published in London by Judd and Glass, of Gray's Inn Road. Judd's partner may have been Glass's son Henry, who became a newspaper editor. Joseph Glass continued to campaign against the use of boys for chimney sweeping, and when he died in 1867 at the age of 75 at his home in Brixton his death was mentioned in the court circular; Queen Victoria had also been concerned about the unhappy experiences of the climbing boys.

Now let Joseph Glass introduce us to the town:

Manningtree is a pleasant market town,
As broad as long, and is of some renown;
And from the river side 'tis plainly seen,
On undulating ground of verdant green.
'Twas by denuded aborigines
Long noted for its woods and many trees;
And centuries have passed since then and now,
When first it had the name of Schidingeou.
Our town, however, is an ancient place,
As we for centuries can its history trace;
But only in an undefined degree,
Some reference here and there we faintly see.
T'was once a haven, and a houseling town,
(In the review of lands 'tis noted down,)
And full three hundred years ago we find

Extensive numbers in the town combined;
And, at the least, seven hundred of our race
Were then residing in this ancient place.
How they contrived and managed their affairs,
And struggled on through all their wants and cares,
We have, indeed, no clear or certain clue –
We fear that mostly they passed roughly through.

66   REMINISCENCES

THE PACKET.

Now fifty years ago, in this our town,

The Inns existed as they're noted down ;

And first, as principal, the *Packet*, where

Was held the Market, and the yearly Fair :

A vessel, was the sign, and under sail,

Flying before a brisk, propitious gale.

The Packet Inn in the centre of Manningtree, from Joseph Glass's book 'Reminiscences of Manningtree and its Vicinity' *published in 1855.*

Joseph Glass remembers back to 1805 when at Whitsuntide Manningtree was a sociable and festive place at the time of the fair, but he was worried by the excessive drinking that went on: "particularly among the working men of the town; and some, but for intoxication, would have maintained a respectable position. Numbers who were victims to this vice I could name, who brought ruin on themselves and families. The poor inebriate has no power to adopt means for self-reclamation. The working men of the town should think seriously of this matter, and arrange, with all due deference, with their masters to be paid in money, and not partly in beer, and request hard cash, instead of tickets on public houses; that the whole of their humble means may be carefully spent at their homes, and appropriated to their domestic comfort".

He says that the larger area of Mistley, "with her ample acres spread, gives all her sons sufficiency of bread" while Manningtree "herself has no lands, except the part on which the township stands".

We can get a glimpse of what living conditions were like in Mistley from the '*Report to the General Board of Health on a Preliminary Enquiry into the Sewerage, Drainage, and Supply of Water, and the Sanitary Condition of the Inhabitants of the Parish of Mistley in the County of Essex*' produced by Alfred L. Dickens, Superintending Inspector, and published in London in 1854.

Mr. Dickens begins his report, as all such reports begin, with a concise description of the place with which he was dealing:

> Mistley is a parish in the union and hundred of Tendring in the northern division of Essex, and is situated about ten miles from Colchester, and between that town and the port of Harwich. The main part of the village is built on the southern shore of the navigable river Stour, along the edge of which are erected spacious quays, to which

vessels of upwards of 300 tons burthen can come up at spring tides. There are some large and well built granaries, but they are now unused. The trade of the place is principally in corn, timber, and coal. The houses of Mistley are mostly built of brick, some coloured, some stuccoed. The houses in Upper Mistley have been run up very lightly, and are arranged irrespective of any general plan. The whole of the parish which originally came under the denomination of the 'village' of Mistley, consisting of the park and quay property, together with all the houses in the main street, was formerly the property of F.H. Rigby, Esq. About ten years ago this property was sold, in lots for building new houses on small freeholds on the higher part of the ground above the main street of the village. This part of the town is now designated Upper Mistley.

Such reports as Mr. Dickens's contain many an interesting snippet of history such as the link between Mistley and the fleet that guarded the country against Napoleon. "The water here used to be considered so good, that the ships of the North Sea fleet in the last war watered from the basin opposite the Thorn Inn. 'The water now would not do for this purpose. Most of the water at lower Mistley is now spoiled, in the witness's opinion, by the cesspools".

In 1875 a writer describes Mistley as "a large village with a quay forming an extension of the port of Manningtree"; Hervey Benham said in 1955 in *Once Upon A Tide* that "nobody walking through the sleepy streets of Manningtree today would suppose more than a score of ships had ever belonged to the place – at any rate till he looked carefully at the substantial Georgian houses, and realised the tale they tell of the different values and rewards of another age".

Ken Rickwood in his *Stour Secrets,* written in 2008, asks "What is Manningtree's secret? Its name is written large on the map, yet it is much smaller than its neighbours".

Manningtree and Mistley in 1897.

Manningtree town about 1975.

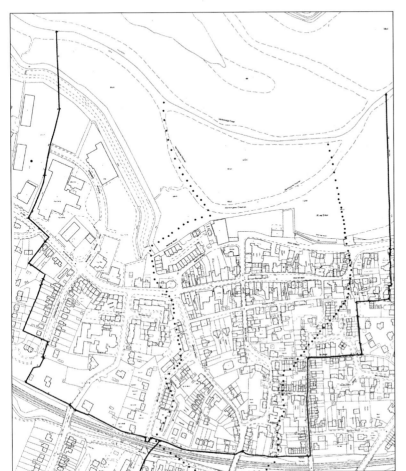

The new Manningtree boundary of 1981 is shown by the black line, and the old boundary taken from a map of 1922 shown with a dotted line.

The Parish Boundaries

Manningtree and Mistley are entwined together, and the parish of Lawford is hard to separate from the two. Manningtree was once known as the smallest town in England – only 17 acres at one time – but whether it actually was the country's smallest town, no one really knows. In the early 1970s the official guide to the town stated that it covered 22 acres.

It seems that the boundary changed from time to time. By the corner of Mill Lane and Brook Street is a plaque in the wall mentioning that in 1871 the boundary between Manningtree and Lawford was close to that location. In 1977,

A parish boundary marker stone dated 1871 which was formerly in the wall of a cottage in Mill Lane, Manningtree. This is now incorporated in the brick wall of a new building on the corner of Mill Lane and Brook Street which was part of the 1970s redevelopment of the area. A metal plaque underneath states: 'This boundary stone was originally built into the wall of the cottage which straddled the line of the parish boundary. On clearance of the site, the stone was removed and has been built into this position for preservation. The original boundary was 10.5 metres (34'.5") west of this position.

when there was insufficient money for such a small town to meet its commitments, Manningtree asked the adjoining parishes for an adjustment of the boundaries to give it a more viable area. At first Manningtree wanted the town limits to reach the railway bridge in Station Road, but Lawford, while agreeing to the boundary being extended a little to the west – to the point where the 'Welcome to Manningtree' sign now stands – declined to give up so large a part of its parish. On the other side of the town the request was for the boundary to reach further east, to No.4 The Walls. These changes were duly made on 1st April, 1981.

Mistley and Lawford surround Manningtree, and at times it is difficult to see where one ends and another begins. The present boundary of the three parishes can be traced, but only part of it can be walked along. Let's try looking where each parish lies by tracing first the Manningtree boundary.

Beginning at the Manningtree end of The Walls, in front of the old Brooks maltings building, now converted into dwellings, the boundary comes in from the middle of the Manningtree channel in the Stour estuary, across the road and up past The Foreman's House on the east side. This house, originally the home of the foreman of the maltings complex, is set back from the road, and is just in Manningtree. The converted maltings and the Kiln Lane estate of new houses are in Mistley. In fact the boundary runs between No.24 Kiln Lane (in Mistley) and No.26 (in Manningtree); crosses Kiln Lane, up past the end of the Central Maltings, and turns sharp right (west) so that No.28 Kiln Lane is just in Manningtree.

The boundary turns sharp left (south) and runs behind the houses in Hilton Close, crosses Malthouse Road, then turns west along the path known as Gasfield. This path is so called because on the Mistley side, by the corner of Oxford Road, was the old gasworks, built in 1840. The gasworks had gone by the 1960s when North Sea gas arrived, and houses stand on the site today.

The boundary then runs along the middle of Oxford Road, with the odd-numbered houses in Mistley and the even numbers in Manningtree. The old boundary ran further west, with the whole of Oxford Road in Mistley. In fact the boundary ran almost through the Wesley School - now the Manifest Theatre.

The boundary continues past the end of Norman Road, then just before crossing the railway line (the bridge is in Mistley) the boundary takes a sharp westerly turn and runs between the edge of the gardens of Railway Terrace and the railway line. It then crosses the road by the bridge, and passes the end of Railway Street. If we follow the boundary along a path here we cross a small stream. The boundary follows the stream under the railway line, on the other side of which it forms the boundary between Lawford and Mistley. There is a point near the bridge, taking Mill Lane under the railway, that is the only place where the parishes of Manningtree, Mistley and Lawford meet.

Crossing Mill Lane, the boundary continues between the gardens and the railway line up to Colchester Road, with Bumblebee Hall in Manningtree and the road bridge in Lawford. The other side of Colchester Road it again runs close to the railway line, but it turns north after No.29 Colchester Road (in Manningtree) and goes to the top end of Queensway, where there is a grass play area which is in Lawford. The boundary comes briefly to Lushington Road, but almost immediately turns west by No.26 (this is in Manningtree) and then runs down the back of the gardens of the even-numbered houses in Lushington Road. Lushington comes from a family of that name that once owned much land in the area.

Manningtree sign – looking towards the town in October 2011.

Then, behind the almshouses, it runs in a north-westerly direction behind Nos. 63 and 65 Station Road, then at the back of the garden of No.67 it turns northerly, leaving No.67 in Manningtree and Victoria Crescent in Lawford. The boundary then crosses Station Road, turns westerly, and runs up to the 'Welcome to Manningtree' sign where the Railex works was before it closed in 2006. The boundary runs along the fence to the sea wall, where it crosses into the middle of the channel to meet the boundary between Essex and Suffolk.

The boundary between Mistley and Lawford follows the brook south from the railway line, crossing Mill Lane almost at its lowest point and then passing close to the 1908 Tendring Hundred Waterworks Company building on the west side and on into open land. It crosses Long Road close to the sign that welcomes you to Lawford and continues due south across fields to Dead Lane, where it turns sharp east and follows the lane to Pedlars Corner. It then meanders across fields, taking in Ford Farm, Dickley Hall, New Hall and Abbotts Hall, to Horsley Cross. The boundary goes just beyond New House Farm, on the other side of the A120. This is the southern-most point of Mistley parish. On the other side, the boundary includes the water tower and Horsley Cross Street, also the old 447 feet high BBC TV mast, built in 1962, and first used on May 22nd of that year. It was decommissioned as a television transmitter in 1986, and is now used for general telecommunications. The boundary envelops Mistley Heath, and the site of the ancient St. Mary's Church. It then snakes across open land to the railway line, through the woods, and out across the mud almost to the middle of the estuary, to Ballast Hill, where a cardinal buoy (indicating shipping should pass on the north side of it) marks the edge of the channel. In the middle of this channel is the Essex Suffolk border. Mistley parish is indeed a large area compared with the tight boundary around its neighbour Manningtree.

The Walls in the 1970s.

Mistley Church by Robert Adam, as seen in an engraving of 1777 after a drawing by G. B. Campion.

Fragments of History

Perhaps Manningtree today is best known to the outside traveller for its railway station, almost exactly half-way between London and Norwich on a line built in the 1840s. But the station is not actually in Manningtree, it is in neighbouring Lawford. The most familiar landmark the local traveller is likely to see is Mistley Towers. Along with the old television mast at the back of Mistley (in fact almost in Bradfield) the Towers, the surviving remnants of a fine 18th-century church, are the most noticed and best remembered.

It was in 1709 that a member of the Rigby family of London inherited much of the land that made up the village of Mistley, including the wharf, later to become the quay. Edward Rigby and his successors are chronicled in Ivan Garwood's excellent *Mistley In The Days Of The Rigbys* published by Lucas Books in 2003. This gives a vivid background not only of the family, their ideas of developing the village into a Spa town, and the history of Mistley Hall, but everyday background life of the village, the quay, the river, and the local industries. It also goes into much detail about the decline of the Mistley estate, and the eventual demolition of Mistley Hall following a series of sales in the 1840s.

Bob Horlock and Mike Fryer in their book *Visiting The Past* published in 2011 show in pictures what Manningtree and Mistley looked like between 1900 and 1925, and from these earlier accounts, and the town and village today, we can see great changes that have taken place over time.

What are the origins of the names Manningtree and Mistley? Going back 1,000 years, Manningtree and Mistley came under the same name of Sciddinchou (various spellings of this old name) in the Domesday Book. The suggestion is made by P.H. Reaney in *The Place Names of Essex* that this could mean 'hill of the shed dwellers'. As for Manningtree itself, there have been many ideas that range from the simple 'many trees' to a place belonging to someone called Mann or Manni. Mistley has been suggested by J. Yelloly Watson in his *Tendering Hundred in the Olden Times* as coming from the Saxon word for the herb basil – mircel – combined with 'ley' meaning pasture, whereas Professor Eilert Ekwall postulates Mistletoe Wood, the old English for mistletoe being 'mistel'.

Witchfinder General

Manningtree is known as the home of the Witchfinder General, Matthew Hopkins, who in the 17th century was responsible for the deaths of so many unfortunate women in this part of the country. Joseph Glass had something to say about Hopkins' doings:

We find by records, that in former years
A most notorious character appears –
Was Matthew Hopkins named, of base renown,
Who long resided in our native town.
By Cromwell's parliament he was empowered,
(A circumstance by some now much deplored!)
And, in plain terms expressed, "to treat about"
To find the poor revolted witches out.
Large numbers by his wiles were guilty found,
And some were strangled, others burnt, or drowned!
While he for each convicted of this crime,
Received full twenty shillings at the time.

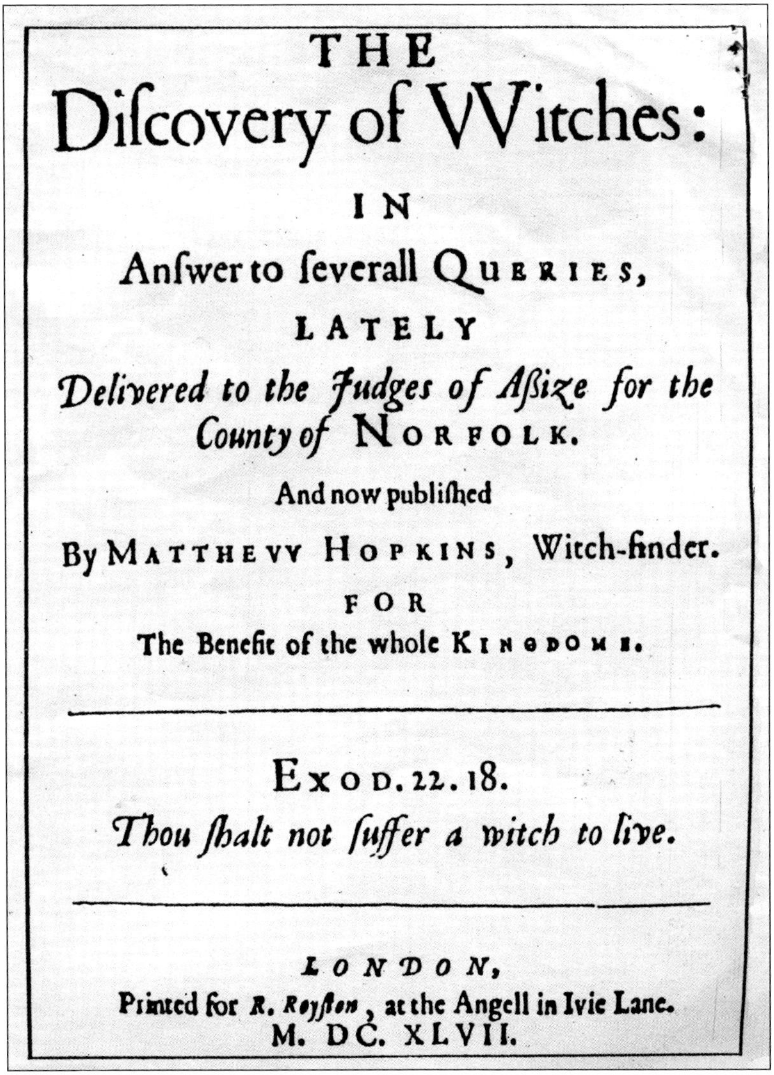

THE
Difcovery of Witches:

IN

Anfwer to feverall QUERIES,

LATELY

Delivered to the Judges of Affize for the
County of NORFOLK.

And now publifhed

By MATTHEVV HOPKINS, Witch-finder.

FOR

The Benefit of the whole KINGDOMI.

EXOD. 22. 18.
Thou fhalt not fuffer a witch to live.

LONDON,
Printed for *R. Royfton*, at the Angell in Ivie Lane.
M. DC. XLVII.

The title page of Matthew Hopkins' book in which he sought to justify his actions.

Unfortunately very little evidence of Matthew Hopkins exists apart from his own book *'The Discovery of Witches: an Answer to severall Queries, lately Delivered to the Judges of Assize for the County of Norfolk, and now published by Matthew Hopkins, Witch-finder, for The Benefit of the whole Kingdom'*. Published as a sort of last resort to allay criticism of his methods, this book provides evidence of how he worked. "The Discoverer never travelled far for it, but in March, 1644, he had some seven or eight of that horrible sect of Witches living in the Towne where he lived, a Towne in Essex, called Manningtree, with divers other adjacent Witches of other townes, who every six weeks in the night (being always a Friday night), had their meeting close by his house, and had their severall solemne sacrifices there offered to the Devill. One of which this discoverer heard speaking to her Imps one night, and bid them goe to another Witch, who was thereupon apprehended, and searched by women who had for many yeares knowne the Devill's marks, and found to have three teats about her, which honest women have not …".

It has been written that he was the son of James Hopkins, minister of Great Wenham in Suffolk, and was born around 1621. Some say he was in the legal profession, and worked in Ipswich. He was about 24 when his witch hunting began in 1645, searching out so-called witches all over East Anglia. He had 68 people put to death in Bury St. Edmunds alone, and 19 hanged at Chelmsford in a single day. Among those hanged at Chelmsford in 1645 were Elizabeth Clarke and Elizabeth Gooding from Manningtree and Anne Leache from Mistley. In the same year Helen Clark, Anne West, Anne Cooper, and Marian Hocket were executed at Manningtree. He was well paid for his work: Aldeburgh paid him £6 for clearing the town of witches, Kings Lynn gave him £15 and Stowmarket £23.

In his *The Discovery of Witches: an Answer to severall Queries'* Hopkins addresses the way in which some of the unfortunate victims died. He poses a question himself:

'Querie 10. But there hath been an abominable, inhumane, and unmerciful tryall of these poore creatures, by tying them and heaving them into the water; a tryall not allowable by Law or conscience, and I would faine know the reasons for that.

Answer. It is not denied but many were so served as had Papps, and floated, others that had none were tryed with them and sunk, but marke the reasons.

For first the Divels policie is great, in perswading many to come of their owne accord To be tryed, perswading them their marks are so close they shall not be found out, so as diverse have come 10 or 12 Miles to be searched of their own accord, and hanged for their labour, (as one Meggs, a Baker did, who lived within 7 miles of Norwich and was hanged at Norwich Assizes for witchcraft), then when they find that the Devil tells them false they reflect on him, and he (as 40 have confessed) adviseth them to be swum, and tels them they shall sinke and be cleared that way, then when they be tryed that way and floate, they see the Devill deceives them again, and have so laid open his treacheries'.

An illustration from Mathew Hopkins' book 'The Discovery of Witches' published in 1647, showing two of his victims and the animals that were said to be their imps.

Much has been written about Hopkins. One book, *Witch-finders: a Seventeenth-Century English Tragedy* by Malcolm Gaskill, published by John Murray, tries to tidy up the story and get at the truth, and is a good start for those researching Hopkins, the man who called himself 'Witchfinder'. The film *Witchfinder General* was made for the cinema in 1968, much of it shot in East Anglia, particularly around Lavenham, and starred Vincent Price as Hopkins, but this was no more than a piece of entertainment.

Hopkins is said to have carried on some of his notorious business at the White Hart in Manningtree, and it is also said that people were killed on The Green in South Street. There is also a story that he died young, and was buried in the old churchyard at Mistley Heath, but there is little hard evidence to support most of these stories. There is, however, a record of his death dated 12th August, 1647, in the Mistley parish register, now to be found in the Essex Record Office, which would suggest that he is indeed buried in the old Mistley churchyard.

All this took place during a period when the country was in an unstable situation. Hopkins came to prominence quickly, but after only a year his methods were questioned, and some say that he was denounced as a sorcerer and hanged. Whatever we do and do not know about him, Hopkins has gone down in history as the Witchfinder General, and he was from Manningtree – he said so himself.

Burglaries

We may not stop to think of thieves at work, but there was a report in The Times on Wednesday 16th June, 1828 which stated:

> In the night of Thursday last the residence of Thomas Nunn, Esq., of Mistley, was broken into and robbed of various articles. The house of William Silk Esq., of the same place, was also entered that night. In both robberies the burglars appear to have been inexperienced hands; their operations were in the dark, it would seem, as they carried away articles of trifling

value compared with those within their reach, and
which were of a more portable description.

The same party, no doubt, entered the premises of Mr.
Harring; but it is presumed they were disturbed by a
dog, as they carried nothing away, but left behind them
a pocket-handkerchief.

Thomas Nunn must have been of Nunn and Co., bankers
in Manningtree, and William Silke is listed as a surgeon in
Silke and Thompson, also of Manningtree. As they both lived
in Mistley, the premises where the handkerchief was left was
probably that of Thomas Herring, a baker in Mistley.

Manningtree market in 2011, in business Friday and Saturdays from early in the morning.

The Markets

The *Universal British Directory* of 1798, describes
Manningtree thus: "It is a dirty town, but has a good market
on Thursday; and one fair the Thursday in Whitsun week"

William White tells us in his directory of 1848 that
Manningtree had a weekly corn market and a Whit Monday
fair. 'Its parish is remarkably small, containing only about
seventeen acres of land and 1,255 inhabitants. A small market
for corn etc. is held every Thursday, in the High Street; and
a fair for toys and pleasure on Whit Thursday.' Joseph Glass

13

picks up the story of the fair as he remembered it when he was a lad, around 1805:

> Some fifty years ago, the townsmen then,
> At Whitsuntide at least, were social men;
> Would actively in various ways prepare,
> To make things pleasant at the coming fair;
> Thus once a year would cheerfully afford
> Their friends a welcome to the festival board;
> Exchange kind words, of past adventures tell,
> Until the time arrive to bid farewell.

He also remembered that the Market Place was a 'rendezvous for boys and men'. He goes on:

> 'Twas here that Cant, and Lilly, sold their fruit;
> And was of various kinds, each taste to suit,
> The cherries ripe, and plums, and mellow pears,
> Raspberries, and currants too, were tempting wares,
> And proved the innocent and sure decoys,
> Of all, as men and women, girls and boys.
> And then as night approached, to see the treasure,
> Of pence and half–pence, in the wooden measure,
> It was a matter of no small surprise,
> To cashless boys, with keen and longing eyes.
> Here aged men as on the bench they sat,
> Would all they knew relate in friendly chat,
> Discoursed full of wars, in France and Spain,
> Of battles, and of numbers that were slain;
> And tell of Boney's great success you see,
> The same of Nelson's victories at sea.

Today the provision market is held twice weekly on a site next to the pond in Brook Street. The market, with stalls for fresh meat, fish, and general food, as well as a seller of eggs, a greengrocer, two dealers in clothes, a general hardware stall, and many other small stalls, starts early on Friday and Saturday mornings.

The brook of Brook Street is unseen here, for it is underground as it makes its way to an outlet in the estuary.

At one time it came into a large pond in the market place which was surrounded by a 3ft. brick wall. Years ago this pond had to be cleaned out every two weeks or so, so that clean water was available for brewery and maltings use.

The present market was established by G.N. Chilvers in 1963, as the plaque on the pond wall says. Gordon Nelson Chilvers opened the fish and chip shop opposite in 1959 and was keen to establish a market on a Friday and Saturday to bring more people into the town. This he did in September, 1963, on land he owned. Later the land was compulsorily purchased by Tendring District Council, but the market continued under different management, changing to Wednesdays and Saturdays. This was not altogether successful, and in 2006 the market reverted to Fridays and Saturdays.

Brooks had a fleet of lorries in 1933, capable of taking loads from 2 to 20 tons.

Transport

What kind of transport system was there before the railway came? *Pigot's Royal National and Commercial Directory* of 1839 reveals a good deal about services by land and water that kept the world on the move.

There was, for instance, the London coach *Defiance* that started from Harwich, called at the White Hart every day at twelve o'clock, then travelled to London via Colchester, Chelmsford and Brentwood. According to the directory, it returned in the late evening, calling at the White Hart 'every night at ten'. Such was the rate of travel that it must be assumed that there were in fact two coaches, running each way.

The coach catered for the long-distance carriage of passengers and light parcels. Operating on the shorter routes there were a number of carriers, including several to Colchester. Benjamin Cant went from his house every Tuesday, Wednesday, Friday and Saturday; Samuel Baker went from his home, presumably at Manningtree, and James Williamson went from Mistley every Monday, Tuesday, Thursday and Saturday; Robert Salter ran from the Rose and Crown every Monday, Wednesday, Thursday and Saturday; and J. Porch operated from the King's Head every Tuesday and Friday. Also advertised: 'A coach to Harwich every evening at half-past 5'. The Rose and Crown is now The Crown, and the Kings Head was on the corner of South Street and the High Street, where Café Rio is today.

A number of carriers operated to Ipswich: William Blyth, from the Red Lion every Tuesday, Thursday, Friday and Saturday; Robert Salter from the Rose and Crown and John Townsend from the King's Head every Tuesday and Friday; and Thomas Tye went from the Packet Inn (now Townsends) every Tuesday.

Then there were two mail carts, one to Harwich from The Cock (in Brook Street) every morning at five and the other to Colchester every night at half-past nine to connect with the Norwich to London Mail.

For heavier goods there were the waggons which travelled at a rather slow pace along the non-surfaced roads of the time. The only one running from Manningtree was Winter's waggon to Long Melford from the White Hart every Tuesday and Friday night. When parcels had to be sent to London or Stowmarket they had to be taken first to the Marlborough Head at Dedham, from which Broom and Winter's waggons ran on Wednesdays and Saturdays.

Another way to transport goods from Mistley and Manningtree to London was by sea from Mistley Quay - 'by way of Harwich', says the directory. The regular trading vessels were the *Sarah Ann, Telegraph, Sisters, Lovely Nancy, Two Brothers, Little John, Manningtree Packet, Deborah, Traveller, Lark, Lydia, Friends' Increase, Friendship, General Elliott, Mary, Despatch*, and two vessels called *Good Intent*, one a sloop and the other a schooner. The *Telegraph* in the list was possibly the vessel of that name owned by Golding Constable, the miller of East Bergholt and Dedham, and the artist's father.

To get to Harwich, perhaps to meet the London packets or the Post Office fast vessels to the continent, there was the passage boat *Sally*, which was owned by John Moor, licensee of the Wherry tavern at Wherry Corner, then in Mistley, but now in Manningtree. Moor was also one of the eight pilots who brought ships up to Mistley Quay; the others were Benjamin, John and Robert Ateen; William Bardale; Thomas Honibal; Richard Saville, and James Thompson.

The Stour from Wherry Corner in 1907.

So life was organised and settled in a routine way in the first part of the 19th century, as it had probably been for centuries before. It was the coming of the railways in the 1840s that changed it all, and speeded up life.

When the railway passed close to Manningtree on its journey from Colchester to Ipswich in 1846, a station was opened almost a mile from the town. "Railway trains 8 times a day to Ipswich, Colchester, London etc. An omnibus from W. Blyth's, High Street, to the station to meet every train". It is generally thought that the railways brought prosperity, but writing nine years after the railway arrived Joseph Glass paints a different picture. He talks of how many people had made an 'ample living' chiefly from the coasting trade, with freights of coal and corn being carried by many ships and with good wages for the sailors, mates, and captains, and the families of the Longs and Howards of the 'fishing trade':

> But now, alas, the Eastern Counties Rail,
> Upsets the town and makes the business fail,
> And how to act our townsmen cannot tell,
> Some cottages will neither let, nor sell,
> All Manningtree, it seems, is out of course,
> And matters as they stand, can scarce be worse.

Manningtree station is in the parish of Lawford. A level crossing for road users was incorporated in the plan, but just before the opening of the line for passengers on 15th June, 1846, an iron girder under-bridge was added 'so that the ordinary traffic of the road will not be interrupted by the gates of the railway,' said the Ipswich Journal. The under-bridge, replaced by a steel one at a later date, and the level crossing, are still in use today.

Two wooden viaducts were built to carry the line over the River Stour to Brantham. These were replaced in 1904 by the present steel structures, but the sawn-off wooden foundations of the old timber bridges can still be found in the river bed. The 1904 bridge on the North Channel leading to Cattawade has a raised section in the ironwork to enable

Manningtree station in 1909, when there were over 20 staff working at the station and goods yard, including the station master Mr. Frederick Swan.

the Stour lighters, immortalised by John Constable, and the Thames sailing barges going as far as Brantham Mill, to get under the railway line when the tide was right. This can still be seen.

The line had to be slightly altered when the new steel viaducts replaced the old timber ones, and for this the owner of Hog Marsh, the spit of land between the two branches of the river, had to be consulted. William Brooks was the owner of this marsh, which was frequently covered by high spring

The reservoir at Manningtree Station that supplied water to the water tower which in turn served the steam trains. A car park now stands on this site.

19

tides, and he used it to graze cattle on. The arrangement with the railway company gave William Brooks the right to drive cattle along the railway line from the level crossing to Hog Marsh, with trains held until the line was clear. Whether this actually happened is not known, but apparently, according to Richard Brooks, the agreement allowed this extraordinary procedure.

Hog Marsh, was technically in Suffolk, and by owning the land William Brooks had the right to vote in Suffolk as well as his home county, Essex. In practice, though, he still only had one vote, and had to choose which county he voted in.

Getting about before the trains was a slow business, as Joseph Glass reminds us:

> To London men could go, in times of old,
> In six and thirty hours, as we've been told;
> Now by express, to London we can go,
> In little better than an hour or so;
> And in a few short minutes, we can send,
> News of importance to a London friend.

The branch line to Harwich was opened in 1854. There was a signal and points box at Manningtree near the level crossing, and another signal box at Mistley station. When the Manningtree North curve, connecting the Harwich branch line to the Ipswich line just short of Cattawade viaduct was opened in 1882, two more signal boxes were added – one at the Mistley end of the curve, and the other at the Ipswich end.

Harold Oxborrow, who in 1985 recalled the Manningtree of his childhood, remembered that at the White Hart "they kept all the horses and traps to go to the Station, and if you wanted a ride there it was threepence, and if you had luggage, that was an extra penny. If you gave the driver a twopenny tip he would have a pennorth of beer and a pennorth of gin".

Today there is a good train service from Manningtree to London, and Manningtree to Ipswich and Norwich.

There is even an early morning train direct to Peterborough for connections to the Midlands and the North.

At Mistley there is one through train in the morning to London, and a shuttle service the rest of the day to Manningtree Station. At 8.02 there is a direct train from Mistley to Cambridge.

The main bus service for both Mistley and Manningtree is a half-hour service to Colchester and Harwich during the day. This is the 103 and 104 from Monday to Saturday, with the 102 on Sundays and Bank Holidays. The 103 route is Harwich Bus Station, Dovercourt High Street & Hospital, Ramsey, Wrabness, Bradfield, Mistley, Manningtree, Lawford, and Ardleigh, to Colchester Bus Station. The 104 route is Harwich Bus Station - Dovercourt High Street & Hospital, Little Oakley, Great Oakley, Wix, Bradfield, Mistley, Manningtree, Lawford, Ardleigh, to Colchester Bus Station.

The Sunday service, the 102, leaves Harwich Bus Station, for Dovercourt High Street & Hospital, Parkeston Quay, Ramsey, Little Oakley, Great Oakley, Wix, Bradfield, Mistley, Manningtree, Lawford, Dedham, Ardleigh, to Colchester Bus Station.

The Bus Station at Harwich, by the railway station, was opened in 1974. Before that there was a bus turn around at Kingsway in Dovercourt. The Eastern National Omnibus Company has origins going back to 1929. The buses today are operated by First Essex Buses Ltd. There are also some bus services to and from Ipswich and Clacton.

The bus service to Colchester, every half hour, is a life-line to many people.

21

Inns and Beerhouses

Writing in 1855, but remembering the area as it was when he was younger, around 1805, Joseph Glass says about Manningtree "Early in life I took particular notice of the sad and degrading effects of intoxication, particularly among the working men of the town; and some, but for intoxication, would have maintained a respectable position".

The Cock Inn was in Brook Street.

Now fifty years ago, in this our town,
The Inns existed as they're noted down;
And first, as principal, the Packet, where
Was held the Market, and the yearly fair:
A vessel was the sign, and under sail,
Flying before a brisk, propitious gale.

Then, referring to the time he was writing, in 1855, he goes on "It is evident that a great deal of immoderate drinking is going on at Manningtree and the neighbourhood, or how could the number of public houses and beer shops be supported?"

Often it is difficult to determine from records and directories which were public houses and which were beer houses, the latter I suppose being places which just sold beer, whereas a pub was more of an Inn. In the confined boundaries of Manningtree in the 18th century there was also William Leech, 'Brandy-dealer'; and Edward Alston, 'Maltster and Brewer'; and the following named public houses in the *Universal British Directory of* 1798:

Rose and Crown in the High Street. 'John Banks, Victualler'.
Packet in the High Street (now Townsends shop). 'Henry Shead, Victualler, and Excise Office'.

Also, though not listed, there was:
Cock Inn in Back Hill (Brook Street).
King's Head at the Market Cross.
Prince Eugene in West Street (which was the High Street).
Red Lion in South Street.
The White Hart in the High Street.

In the 19th century this list of pubs was added to by the addition of:

Lifeboat at the top of Wherry Corner at Forge Cottage.
Anchor of Hope (or just Anchor) in South Street by the corner of North Street.

Saddlers Arms in Quay Street.

Walnut Tree at the top of Brook Street.

White Lion in South Street.

Foresters Arms in South Street.

Rifleman run by James Earthy in South Street.

Princess Alexandra at the top of Brook Street run by James Cook

There were four beer retailers listed in Manningtree in 1886: Alfred Sargent in South Street; Emily Frost in the High Street; William Tice in Oxford Road; and Mrs. Kezia Vincent - listed as 'beer retailer and blacksmith' in Brook Street. To add to these there was 'Ale and Porter Merchants' Goody & Son in South Street.

It seems at one time in the second half of the 19th century the Rose and Crown changed its name to The Cricketers Arms, and then back to The Crown Hotel. In the 1886 list is the following – 'James Hibberd, White Hart, hotel and inland revenue office, High Street'. For those not wanting to imbibe, there was always George Goddard's Coffee Tavern in South Street.

The Skinners Arms in the 19th century was outside the Manningtree boundary, actually in Lawford, and that is why it, and The Flag Inn at the bottom of Colchester Road, and The Wherry on Wherry Corner (actually in Mistley) are not listed.

In 1902, Kelly's directory listed the following 'Public Houses, Inns, and Taverns' and 'Beer Retailers' in Manningtree:

Public houses:

The Crown. George Abbiss, High Street, Manningtree

King's Head. W.E.A. Norman, High Street, Manningtree

The Packet. Frank James Basil Curtis, High Street, Manningtree

Red Lion Inn. Samuel Woodbine, South Street, Manningtree

White Hart. William Culling, High Street, Manningtree

The Anchor at the top of Mistley Hill on the Harwich Road. November 2011.

Beer retailers:
Charles Calver, South Street Manningtree
James Cook, South Street, Manningtree
Mrs. Emily Frost, High Street, Manningtree
Jonathan Nightingale, Station Road, Manningtree
James Sage, South Street, Manningtree
George Vincent, Brook Street

By the 1920s the pubs listed in Kelly's Directory as in Manningtree are:
Crown Hotel
Red Lion
Skinners Arms (still in Lawford at this time, though listed as Manningtree)
Swan
White Hart

In *Kelly's Directory of 1937* we have in Manningtree:
Annie Liveridge, Beer Retailer, 33 South Street, Manningtree
Crown Hotel. Mrs. Townsend, 51 High Street, Manningtree
Red Lion Inn. Percy Calton, 42 South Street, Manningtree
The Swan. Mrs. Laura Vincent, Brook Street, Manningtree
White Hart Hotel, High Street, Manningtree

Not actually in Manningtree at this time:
Skinners Arms. Samuel Seager, Station Road, Manningtree.

Today, 2012, they all still exist, except that The Swan is now the Nirala Tandoori Restaurant and Bar, and Liveridges is long gone.

Listed as in Mistley in the 18th century:
Three Cups. This was on the Bromley Road, and closed in 1772.
Cross Inn at Horsley Cross
Thorn in Mistley itself.

In the 19th century:
Welcome Sailor
White Horse to the west of The Thorn
Anchor
Cross Inn at Horsley Cross
Globe on the Quay
Grapevine on the Quay
Essex Arms
Lord Denman
Pilot on the Quay by Batter Pudding Hill
Swan to the west of the Swan Basin
Staring Dog at Kerridge's Cut.
Stour to the east of the Swan Basin
Waggon and Horses in New Road
Wheelwrights, later to be The Blacksmiths' Arms, at Mistley Heath.

Besides 'Taverns and Public Houses', there is separately listed 'Retailers of Beer', of which there were in the 19th century:
Jane Avis
George Cant (also a carpenter and joiner)
William Frost
James Goddard
James Hayward

Robert Henley
Edward Ireland (also a carrier)
Jeremiah Allan
John Roden Johnson
William Manning of Horsley Cross Road
John Moore
Samuel Paskell
Walter Taylor of Mistley Heath (also a blacksmith)
John Wyncoll Baxter (also a blacksmith and ironmonger)

'Public Houses, Inns, and Taverns' and 'Beer Retailers' in Mistley in 1902:
Public houses
Lord Denman. Thomas Hunneyball, Mistley
Thorn Inn. Edgar T. Berry, Mistley
Wagon and Horses. William Worthy Holmes, New Road, Mistley

Beer retailers in Mistley in 1902:
Mrs. I. Allen, Mistley
Richard Barton, Mistley Heath

Always a warm welcome from
Andy and Margaret Wingham at . . . . .

The Lord Denman
Public House

Come and visit the Aviary and Rock Pool
Children's TV. Room
BECKFORD ROAD :: MISTLEY
Telephone: Manningtree 2944

A 1970s advertisement for the Lord Denman public house.

Joseph Liggins, High Street, Mistley
Samuel James Mullett, Mistley
John George Tice, Oxford Road, Mistley
Arthur Wilson, Mistley

By the 1930s all we have is:
Anchor run by William Edward Cook
Blacksmiths Arms at Mistley Heath
Cross Inn at Horsley Cross run by George Newton
Lord Denman run by George Hunneyball
Thorn Hotel
Waggon And Horses in New Road

Also there was Frank Killick, Beer Retailer in Oxford Road. And once again for those who preferred it, Edgar Harry Baldwin, grocer and tobacconist in Harwich Road, Mistley, provided teas and refreshments.

As always, Joseph Glass has something to say as to what went on in pubs and taverns:

> On business matters: they attend at first,
> Then take a glass or two to quench their thirst.
> Half pints they quaff, of ale, or stout, or porter,
> And smoke, and drink their rum and gin and water.
> Meanwhile their business is so much extended –
> 'Tis hard indeed, to tell when't will be ended-
> 'Tis night! – one leaves for home with staggering gait,
> But is not seen, as it is getting late.

The Name's The Same

In spite of all the changes that have occurred in the past, there are still some families that have lived in the Manningtree and Mistley area for many generations. The oldest yet found is a reference in *The History of Harwich Harbour* by Carlyon Hughes of 1388 in the customs accounts of the Port of Orwell. "The cog *Anne* of Harwich leaves with cloth belonging to John Lucas of Manningtree".

THE RED LION.

We now survey the Inn that is the last,

'Tis strongly built, and raised in years long past ;

A Lion was the sign, a rampant beast,

With open mouth, who seem'd inclined to feast

On harmless animals, disposed to stray,

Or those, who thoughtlessly might cross his way.

The Red Lion in South Street from Joseph Glass's book of 1855.

Some of the tradesmen listed in Pigot's directory in 1839 had surnames that we still associate with the area today. Among them are:

Ainger	James, boot and shoe maker and shopkeeper in Mistley.
Constable	Abraham, coal merchant in Mistley
Cook	James, butcher and earthenware dealer in Mistley. John, baker in Manningtree.

Honibal	Thomas, pilot to Mistley Harbour. (several spellings of this name).
Norman	Edward, maltster, corn and coal merchant, Manningtree.
Parsons	William, plumber, painter and glazier in Manningtree.
Paskell	Thomas, baker in Manningtree. John, carpenter and builder in Mistley. Susan, grocer and draper in Manningtree.
Pittock	James, basket maker in Manningtree.
Saxby	William, hairdresser in Manningtree.

Jack Francis stoking the retorts at Manningtree gas works in 1956. When Jack retired he became part-time caretaker at the gas shop in South Hill.

Obnoxious Odours and Stinking Water

It is hard to imagine what daily life was like in Manningtree and Mistley, when the only way to transport people and goods locally was by horse-drawn coaches, chaises, gigs, carts, waggons etc., with their resulting deposits on the unmade-up roads; when the smell from the gas works in Manningtree spread across the town; from the mud at low tide and raw sewage that entered the river; the strong aroma of the tannery behind the Skinners Arms; and the smoke from chimneys and trains that drifted in the air. If the wind was from the North East, then the added aroma from Mr. Earthy's boat, moored off Mistley where he melted fat to make candles, must have been noticed when he began operations in 1875. Later, when the British Xylonite factory across the river was making celluloid, a northerly wind filled Manningtree and Mistley with a not-so-nice chemical smell – something that continued right up to the 1990s. Added to this were the businesses and factories – the brewery in Manningtree, the maltings in Mistley, and much more besides.

D. Jennings Smith, in his *Manningtree: Study and Proposals* of 1970, describes Manningtree as "a small town with an ancient street pattern, many fine medieval, seventeenth and eighteenth-century buildings mainly in the High Street and South Street".

He describes Mistley as "probably the finest example in Essex of the intermixture of living and working practised in the 19th century and the equal care bestowed on the design of buildings for both uses. The combination of malting, a semi-rural industry, with a small town closely linked to open country and the sea provides a uniquely satisfactory visual environment where the industrial buildings (many having archaeological importance) form a vital part of the town's character".

There was a time, however, when different descriptions were being expressed about living conditions in Mistley. With the population increasing fast in the 19th century it was the state of the sanitation that caused most concern. In 1841 there were 976 people living in 223 houses, and ten years later the 1851 census revealed that the population had risen to 1,516, while the number of houses had risen to 368, partly due to the sale of the Rigby estate in 1844 having resulted in many plots of land being sold for building purposes. New houses had been built, particularly in Upper Mistley.

Alfred Dickens's *Report to the General Board of Health on a Preliminary Enquiry into the Sewerage, Drainage, and Supply of Water, and the Sanitary Condition of the Inhabitants of the Parish of Mistley*, published in 1854, gives us a stark picture of what everyday life was like. Quoting the evidence of John Thomas Ambrose, one of the churchwardens, a resident of Mistley Green, and formerly steward of the Mistley estate under the Rigby's, the report says of the local roads:

> The main streets of the villages of Upper and Lower Mistley are composed of parish roads, under the management of the surveyors of highways, and the turnpike road from Harwich to Colchester, which is under the management of that Trust. There are private roads in the village of Upper Mistley, contiguous to which houses are erected; but these roads have not yet been dedicated to the parish. They have never been formally offered to the parish, and [the witness] believes if they were, the parish would decline to take them. They have been made on the freehold of those who have purchased building lots.
>
> The weather being remarkably fine at the period of my inspection, these roads were not quite so bad as they sometimes are. I am told they are in a wretched state after rain, and in the winter, almost impassable. There is not the slightest provision for surface drainage; and all the slops and house refuse are thrown out of the houses on the road, back or front. They are consequently in a very dirty state, even in their least offensive condition,

when I saw them. The want of proper surface paving in the yards and courts – of Upper Mistley more especially – is very apparent.

Writing of the water supply, Dickens was noncommittal about the various sources of water, but witnesses had told of serious problems that were probably not immediately apparent to outsiders. The water supply came from three separate sources, the springs at Upper Mistley, a spring in the park from which the water was carried to some houses, and from wells either private or public. There was also a well on the shore at the north-west end of Mistley, but this was likely to be flooded by salt water at spring tides. Some of the inhabitants, he was told, complained of having had their water supply cut off when the railway cutting was excavated.

The water supply to a cottage in California Road was analysed and considered to be objectionable because of the quantity of vegetable and animal organisms floating in it. Another specimen from a well in the yard of a cottage was declared to be 'rendered impure from the percolation of drains', and the woman who lived in the cottage said that the water 'sometimes smells of the privy, and with a hot sun on the well it is very filthy'. No wonder two gentlemen who were questioned declared that at times the water from their wells or reservoirs was 'utterly undrinkable'. The analyst's description of one sample is pretty damning, but it was not described as undrinkable:

The village pump close to The Green in Mistley.

> The water has a disagreeable smell, and on being decanted, showed floating particles and animalcules visible to the eye (crustacean). On the water being allowed to stand, a sediment was obtained, which, examined by the microscope, showed numerous vegetable and animal organizations.

The water supply for the village was originally obtained from Upper Mistley, where it came from springs in the area behind California Road. This is the water that once found its way to the beak of the swan in the Swan Basin.

Mention is made of good supplies of watercress here; although no reservoir remains. A concrete channel with small weirs to retain the water levels was constructed, just after 1907, by the Rose family. Ian Rose used to collect good watercress from here until the 1990s. Today the water is all piped away.

Remarking that many children and young people in Mistley were dying from preventable diseases, Mr. Dickens observed that the constant permeation of cesspool and other refuse into the gravelly subsoil under and around the houses and wells was the most apparent cause of the illnesses, and deaths. He noted that it was common for cesspools to be right next to the tanks in which drinking water was collected.

Pointing out how the deficiencies of the drainage system caused illness, he quotes the evidence of Thomas Peat, who was surgeon to the Union, which ran the workhouse at nearby Tendring. Peat said that there had been an epidemic of 'diarrhoea of a choleraic character' in Mistley, and the spread of this disease had been made worse by the dirty state of the houses, both inside and out.

This was the 'dipping well' in the High Street where once upon-a-time people could 'dip' their buckets in to a small basin to get drinking water, or hang their pail on the iron rod that can still be seen, to fill up.

Having made his general observations on the state of things Mr. Dickens took a closer look at parts of the parish, and it is here that his descriptions become most graphic. First of all he takes a look at The Green, an area that today might be thought idyllic; his description of it is anything but, mentioning in particular a row of houses whose privies abutted on the 'back lane'. Those privies had cesspools that were allowed to overflow into a private watercourse flowing down from the park.

> This watercourse runs into the water meadow opposite the church, and is there used for irrigation. The more solid portion of the refuse lies at the mouth of the drain, poisoning the surrounding atmosphere with its effluvia. Very great complaints are made of this nuisance.

Mr. Dickens goes on to say that in Upper Mistley the cesspool system was even worse than that in the lower part of the town.

> The cesspool is generally so placed as to be within a few yards of the well from which the drinking water is obtained, and above its level. There is almost a total absence of house drains of any kind; and even where a sink is in existence there is no pipe from it, and the refuse from washing and other household purposes is thrown out at the back door and allowed to sink into the gravel.
> All slops from the cottage I examined are thrown out at the back door, and drain by open gutter into a small tub. This tub is filled with black refuse, the smell of which is very disagreeable. The privies adjoin the back kitchen, a closet from which is next the covered ash pit. These privies are emptied about twice a year. One of the inhabitants, a woman, complains much of the smell of the privy.

35

Alfred Dicken's 1854 Report.

PUBLIC HEALTH ACT
(11 & 12 Vict. Cap. 63.)

REPORT

TO THE

GENERAL BOARD OF HEALTH

ON A

PRELIMINARY INQUIRY

INTO THE SEWERAGE, DRAINAGE, AND SUPPLY OF
WATER, AND THE SANITARY CONDITION
OF THE INHABITANTS

OF THE PARISH OF

MISTLEY,

IN THE COUNTY OF ESSEX,

By ALFRED L. DICKENS, Esquire, C.E.,

SUPERINTENDING INSPECTOR.

LONDON:
PRINTED BY GEORGE E. EYRE AND WILLIAM SPOTTISWOODE,
PRINTERS TO THE QUEEN'S MOST EXCELLENT MAJESTY.
FOR HER MAJESTY'S STATIONERY OFFICE.

1854.

California Road had presumably been developed not long before Mr. Dickens arrived to investigate the state of its houses; the name is quite a common one and usually indicates an area that was being developed at the time of the California Gold Rush of 1849. One might, therefore, have expected the arrangements to be rather better than they were. In one cottage, occupied by a carpenter, Dickens found the privy in the workshop. The carpenter's wife 'complained much of the smell, and also of the water. The stench is very offensive'. Perhaps we should not be surprised to read that the woman spoke of her sickly health, and said that her child had been seized with violent vomiting that very morning.

Adding to the 'stench' described above were certain cargoes on the quay, such as manure from London. Mr. Charles Tovell told the inquiry that large quantities of manure for agricultural purposes were brought from London by barges that discharged their cargoes on the quay, where the 'muck' sometimes remained for weeks before the farmers removed it. The stench was well nigh intolerable. It probably consisted of the sweepings of the London streets together with the clearings of the stables, but for the Essex farmers it was a very useful cargo. Mr. Dickens was told that this manure cost at Mistley about £10 per barge-load of 40 tons.

One witness told Mr. Dickens that he believed the farmers would gladly purchase the sewage manure if it were 'properly manufactured for their purposes', and that statement was backed up by William Freeborn, one of the local Mistley farmers.

All this adds up to Mistley being an unhealthy place at that time, with people of all ages dying from diseases that could be prevented by proper sanitation and unpolluted supplies of drinking water. To underline his recommendation that a Local Board should be appointed to carry out the provisions of the Public Health Act of 1848, Mr. Dickens printed as an appendix to his report a list of all the 251 people who had died in the ten-year period since 1844, giving the cause of death in each case. A few died of old age, but many were the babies

*Rigby cottages facing
The Green.*

and young children who died of convulsions, inflammation of chest, bowels or stomach, typhus fever or tuberculosis. The list of deaths for 1849-50 is reproduced below, with an approximation to a present day medical description of the cause of death given in brackets.

E. Sharp, male 11 years. Scarlatina maligna [Sore throat and rash like scarlet fever].
G. Stevens, male 5 months. Infantile remittent fever [possibly malaria].
M.A. Hughs, female 33 years. Tabes mesenterica [TB of lymph glands in abdomen].
L. Carrington, female 62 years. Dysentery and exhaustion.
G. W. Chissell, male 2 years. Diarrhoea collapse.
C Mason, male 4 months. Pneumonia.
R. Allen, female 2 years. Convulsion fit [Possibly epilepsy].
A. Hammond, male 1 year. Pneumonia.
R. Wright, female 11 weeks. Atrophy [Emaciation].

The Lane behind Rigby cottages.

G Pannifer, male 45 years. Phthisis [Pulmonary tuberculosis].

R. T. Paskell, male 2 years. Hydrocephalus [Water on the brain].

E. Seagers, male 10 weeks. Thrush [Candida of mouth or genitals].

M.A. Page, female 6. months Diarrhoea.

J. Angier, male 2 months. Pneumonia.

E.B. Marven, male 4 years. Croup.

H.W. Abbott, male 6 months. Dysentery.

M.A. Carrington, female 9 months. Accidentally burnt by clothes catching fire.

E. Scott, female 64 years. Affection of the heart.

R. Tovell, female 22 years. Exhaustion after parturition [Childbirth].

J. Tovell, male 1 day. Malformation of the heart.

F.T. Folkard, male 20 years. Phthisis [Pulmonary tuberculosis].

J. Wright, male 32 years. Psoas Abscess [Abscess on the loin muscles].

T. Cant, male 1 year. Mirasmas [Malnutrition caused by starvation].
A. Durrant, female 66 years. Apoplexy [Stroke].
S. Tovell, male 80 years. Bronchitis.
S. Siggers, female 7 years. Fever and effusion on the brain [Water on the brain].
D. Lee, male 18 years. Diarrhoea and cramp from drinking ditch water.
E.C. Pearce, female 10 months, Bronchitis.
J. Stock, male 28 years. Pneumonia.
M.A. Watts, female 24 years. Typhus fever [Infectious disease caused by lice or fleas].

This picture of squalor and disease caused by lack of proper sanitation was not peculiar to Mistley. Something very similar could be found in most towns and villages at that time, compounded by an expanding population. What this report does show is the growing concern at the situation, and a will on the part of some people at least to remedy it in the countryside just as people like Sir Joseph Bazalgette were tackling similar problems in London and elsewhere.

The River Stour   3

The tidal water at Manningtree and Mistley is known locally
as 'the river', but in fact it is an arm of the sea, the estuary of
the Stour, and the tide creeps up twice a day covering the mud
banks and filling the river from shore to shore. When the tide
is out, there is no water at Manningtree to float boats, only
a foot or so of ebbing tide mixed with fresh water coming
down the two channels from the upper Stour, from Sudbury
and beyond.

   The Stour begins its journey to the sea at West Wickham
in Cambridgeshire, running past Haverhill, Clare and Sudbury
and becoming an estuary at Cattawade, just above Manningtree.
For much of its course it forms the county boundary between
Suffolk and Essex.

   This end of the Stour estuary was once a working river,
with commercial shipping and busy fishermen. It is recorded

*The River Stour at
Manningtree in days
gone by.*

41

by Carlyon Hughes in his *The History of Harwich Harbour* that "In 1571 Harwich possessed three ships of the burden of 100 tons, three of 80 tons and others are recorded down to a burden of only eight tons. Manningtree at this time possessed three ships of 40 tons".

The sea was certainly the benefactor of Manningtree and Mistley up to the 19th century. The one-time prosperity is reflected by the extensive Georgian fronts on what are often very old cottages and houses. All that wealth was threatened by the arrival of the Eastern Union Railway, constructed to link Ipswich with the Eastern Counties Railway at Colchester, according to Joseph Glass, who as ever had a comment to make on the situation:

> Our native town, some fifty summers past,
> Assumed an aspect of a different cast;
> As former plans were set aside and changed
> By railway schemes – now altered and deranged.
> For numbers then an ample living made,
> Arising chiefly from the coasting trade.
> Then large continuous freights of coals and corn,
> Were to and from, by numerous vessels borne;
> And sailors then, and mates, and captains too,
> Good wages had, and all were well to do.

Two years after the railway arrived in 1846 William White in his directory for Manningtree and Mistley lists more than 40 ship's masters and records that 'the number of vessels belonging to the port is now about 460, and their aggregate amount of tonnage nearly 37,000 tons.' He goes on to say that 'in 1847, eight ships brought here 5,447 quarters of wheat from the Baltic [a quarter is a ¼ of a hundredweight and was the common measure of grain], and in the same year there were large importations of oil cake, deals, etc.', and records an 'extensive trade in corn, coal, timber and fish', but provides no record of how many fishermen there were.

The Master Mariners listed in the 1848 directory were:

Samuel Anderson	John Lilley
Joseph Brown	Jasper Lucas
John Burgess	Thomas Lucas
Thomas Carrington	Fredrick Maulding
Jasper Chipperton	James Maynard
Charles Chisnall	John Morley
C. J. Chisnall	William Noye
Robert Cooper	Isaac Osborne
Samuel Crisp	John Pear
James Davis	Daniel Price
Samuel Eade	Samuel Proom
John Edgley	Robert Purdy
William Forster	Jasper Richardson
Jacob Gobell	Stephen Russell
Robert Hebble	James Spendley
Jasper Howard	William Strutt
William Humphries	Charles Thompson
Oliverer Hurran	Robert Thompson
William Jeffries	William Thompson
William Jenkins	William Totham
Robert Lawrence	James Went
Joseph Lever	James Wright

A drawing of Mistley Quay c1930, by young Harry Fuller who lived in Alma Square in Manningtree and worked for Brooks. In the water-colour belonging to Michael Hubbard, we see the sprittie Orion *which belonged to William Green of the roller mill at Brantham, and the steamer* Mistley *which was built at Mistley by F. W. Horlock in 1922. On the extreme left is Brooks's own sailing barge* Swan.

Some of the ship-owners were listed:

Thomas Green	John Moor
Richard Horlock	Robert Page
George Howard	Thomas Taylor
James Howard	Charles Tovell
John Jessup	George Tovell
Benjamin Long	Samuel Tovell
Fredrick Maulding	Samuel Tovell Junior
John May	William Wymark

Merchants listed were:

Robert Allen	Edward Norman
Edward Alston	Joseph Page
Daniel Constable Alston	Robert Page
Charles Bawtree	William Shansfield
Edward Bowles	Charles Shepherd
John Baxter	Henry Squirrell
William Folkard	Charles Tovell
William Harris	Samuel Tovell
Jasper Howard	James Vice
John Long	William Wymark
John Mann	James Wright

Four sailing barges at Mistley Quay.

Sailing Barges

To many people Mistley is inseparable from the sailing barge, sales publicity for the apartments on Mistley Quay tending to show the scene with a couple of barges alongside. Many famous barges were owned in Mistley and manned by Mistley men. Even now the *Victor*, built at Ipswich in 1895, is often seen moored at David Foster's yard.

The name of Horlock is synonymous with Mistley and barges. There was a Richard Horlock among the local ship-owners in 1848, though the family had come to Mistley not many years earlier from the Rettenden area of South Essex. In the course of the 19th century the Horlock family did well, and the Mistley economy thrived with them. Those who wish to know more of the family's fortunes can read Chubb Horlock's account of their success, written down by his son Bob and published in *Mistleyman's Log*, an enthralling account of barges and barge racing and the result of a notable father-and-son partnership. In 2009 Bob Horlock and Ron Weyda published *The Racing Horlocks*, a comprehensive account of the racing achievements of the Horlock family from 1868 to 1971.

It was Richard Horlock who entered his *Excelsior*, built at Ipswich by William Bayley, in the new class for large barges introduced into the Thames match in 1868. It is said that Richard's two sons had time to tar only one side of the barge in preparation for the race, the other side being still dirty when she sailed home first in her class. It was the beginning of a long run of racing successes for the family.

One of Richard's grandsons, Frederick William, built up a large fleet of barges and larger vessels, and also reintroduced shipbuilding to Mistley in the years after the First World War. Not content with barge-owning, he formed F.W. Horlock's Ocean Transport Company and acquired deep-sea tramps that traded worldwide; needless to say, they were much too large to visit Mistley, where the company's office was situated in the High Street. These big vessels included the *Mary Horlock* and the *Coralie Horlock*, named after F.W.'s daughters.

In 1919 he began to lay out a shipyard on land to the east of the quay and started building steel ships. The first from the new yard was the steam coaster *Phaeacian*, which was launched in 1920, followed in 1922 by a similar vessel named *Mistley*. This vessel ran aground at Deal in 1927, and had to be dug out of the sand by a small army of men before she could be re-floated on the next high tide. This event made the national newsreels in the cinema. "SS Mistley Driven Ashore on Christmas Eve".

The first steel sailing barge to come off the Horlock yard was the *Repertor* in 1924, followed the next year by the *Portlight*, and in 1926 by the *Xylonite*, which was used to carry barrels of acid to the British Xylonite factory at Brantham. The steamer *Arete*, at 898 gross tons, the biggest vessel ever built at Mistley, was laid down alongside the *Portlight* in 1925. It is said that the plates were brought from Lowestoft in the firm's barges. Other barges built in the same yard were the *Adieu, Reminder, Resourceful* and *Blue Mermaid*, the latter launched in 1930, the last sailing barge to be built. The *Blue Mermaid* met a violent end, being blown up by a mine off Clacton during the Second World War. The *Resourceful* was converted into a motor coaster in 1933. The barges built at Horlock's yard were distinctive in design and could be easily recognised by the barge fraternity when seen at sea; they were built to carry a large cargo, but they were also fast.

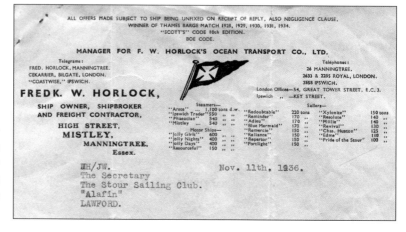

Horlock's letter heading of 1936. The letter is from the Stour Sailing Club collection and is about a dispute in a sailing race.

Frederick Horlock described himself on his notepaper in the 1930s as 'Ship Owner, Shipbroker, and Freight Contractor'. His letter heading listed four steamers: *Arete*, *Ipswich Trader*, *Phaeacian* and *Mistley*; four motor ships, *Jolly Girls*, *Jolly Days*, *Jolly Nights* and *Resourceful*; and the sailing barges *Redoubtable*, *Reminder*, *Adieu*, *Blue Mermaid*, *Remercie*, *Reliance*, *Repertor*, *Portlight*, *Xylonite*, *Resolute*, *Millie*, *Revival*, *Charles Hutson*, *Edme* and *Pride of the Stour*. He also proudly boasted on the letter heading 'Winner of Thames Barge Match 1928, 1929, 1930, 1931, and 1934'.

Frederick William took a keen interest in barge racing and personally superintended the fitting out of craft for the matches, in which Horlock barges had considerable success. One of the most successful skippers was Captain Alfred Horlock, who was described by Frank Carr in his book *Sailing Barges* as "a splendid specimen of a sailorman, a man of iron nerve and great determination". To illustrate his extraordinary physical strength, Frank Carr tells a story of how on one occasion he had spent the day humping sacks of wheat on his back to load his barge, then sailed her about five miles downriver and anchored; he rowed the heavy barge's boat back to Mistley over the ebb tide to go to a dance; danced until early in the morning; then rowed back to his barge over the last of the flood, got under way at once and sailed to London.

Alfred's nephew, also christened Alfred but better known throughout his life as Chubb, enjoyed considerable success in the latter-day barge matches with crews drawn from Mistley. At the time he first went to sea there were 14 or 15 Horlocks in barges.

The Stour Navigation

Freights were sometimes transferred from seagoing vessels to lighters for transport up the Stour Navigation. The stretch of river between Cattawade and Sudbury was made navigable in 1709 with 15 locks, and there is a suspicion that the river might have been first made navigable in the previous century. The laden barges were often poled on a flooding tide along

A very low tide on September 30ᵗʰ 2011. This means the spring tides will be extra high.

Thorn Reach, round the channel to Cattawade and on to Flatford, Dedham, and Sudbury.

According to John Boyes and Ronald Russell, authors of *The Canals of Eastern England*, in 1710 there was an agreement with one John Ricklingham, who was master of the *Ryall* of Whitby, to carry coal from Sunderland to Manningtree at 24 shillings per chaldron. At Manningtree the coal was transferred to barges and sent on up river. [A chaldron was the common measure for coal and one chaldron equals 36 bushels, a bushel being 36.369 litres in dry measure].

The main cargoes of the Stour navigation were coal and timber, with corn, malt, and bricks on the return journey. At one time Allen's brickworks at Ballingdon alone operated a fleet of 22 barges. The navigation suffered severely from railway competition, though lighters continued to work until 1916 to and from Sudbury, and about 1928 from Mistley to Dedham.

Today only a few working ships come up to Mistley Quay, where aggregate and other cargoes are unloaded; none come to Manningtree. The area is now primarily the preserve of the recreational sailor. In the summer months, April to October, the estuary is home to boats attached to the Stour Sailing Club, which administers the hundred or so moorings on behalf of the Harwich Haven Authority. During the winter months most boats are lifted out and either taken home by their owners or stored in the Stour Sailing Club compound next to Jewsons' yard.

Thomas Howard who transferred eight of his fishing boats from Manningtree to Grimsby in the 1850s.

Manningtree To The Humber

In days gone by there were several people making a living from fishing at Manningtree, including the Woollard, Porter and Lucas families. They fished locally, as well as going many miles in search of a catch. Jack Lucas remembers going up the Orwell, where the crew would stay in the boat for several days catching as much as they could; and Chubb Horlock tells in '*Mistleyman's Log*' of the Woollard family setting crab pots off Walton.

One family, the Howards, went even further. The Howard family of Manningtree built and owned boats large and small in the 1830s and 1840s. When the railway companies were beginning to develop Grimsby as a fishing port they employed agents to scour the southern ports and the Thames estuary to persuade fishermen to migrate to Grimsby. The Great Northern Railway Company offered a remunerative daily market with guaranteed earnings, no dock dues, and free rail transport of their fish to the markets. They found only one person interested, Thomas Howard of Manningtree, who moved eight of his large fishing boats, the *British Rover*, *Emma*, *Howard*, *Laurel*, *Liberty*, *Marquis*, *Mary* and *Success*, to Grimsby. Those that went with them included John Allen and William Mudd, skippers of two of the boats, and Harrison Mudd, a cabin boy.

Fishing In The River

Tony Jiggins eel fishing with fyke nets in Thorn Reach one early misty September morning in 2011.

There have been many changes in the river since the days when fishermen went after eels, flounders, gorebills (garfish), mullet, smelts, and occasionally sea trout and inshore herring. Also on offer were winkles, whelks and eel pouts. William Pittock tells of the ribbon weed that grew thickly on the mud years ago (it disappeared in the 1930s, just after the Spartina grass appeared in 1929) and washed up into heaps on the shore. It was collected in tumbrels by local farmers, and in wheel-barrows by local gardeners who used it on their allotments.

Several people recalled Mrs. Lucas walking round the town selling live dabs and flounders from a basket, and Jack Lucas remembers going as far as East Bergholt selling fish and winkles. Jack told how during the Second World War the estuary was patrolled by fast motor boats at night, and though he could go fishing down the river he had to be home by six. If not ashore by the appointed time, he said, the fast patrol boats from Harwich would come after you and ask questions. And if

Jim Pittock with a flounder he had just netted to add to those already in his boat. This photograph was taken in 1973, when flat fish could easily be found in the channels.

you failed to stop they would fire above your heads, which for a young boy was very frightening, he remembered.

Several members of the Porter family went out fishing and wildfowling, and built boats. One, Dod Porter, who lived in Quay Street overlooking the river, was also the local chimney sweep. When he died in 1968 it was said that as a sweep he was a craftsman of the highest order, and he shot as well as he swept, competing at Bisley, the National Shooting Centre in Surrey. The old cottages in Quay Street disappeared around the late 1960s; the present houses being built on their site.

The river had more fish in it than it has now. Fred Woollard used to go after eels. During a conversation with the writer in 1970, Fred said that he had been born in Cattawade in 1907, and long before he left school he used to go eel babbing with his father often until quite late in the evening. "I used to get in school next day half asleep". At 13 years of age he worked in a baker's shop then in existence near Wherry Corner. "I used to go round with a man with a horse and cart delivering bread round Brantham, Bergholt and Manningtree," he said. "The horse bit me twice. I had been on that about a year, father was

51

Tony Jiggins took this picture of Alan 'Dusty' Miller with his smoking apparatus full of eels on the allotments off Trinity Road in 2010.

seriously ill, his second bout of pleurisy and pneumonia. The doctor said there was only one thing would get him better, to be continuously out in the open air". So Fred packed in his job and he and his father set off in a converted ship's lifeboat for a spell of fishing in the Walton Backwaters. "We rigged up a peter net sixty yards long, and at two hours after high water we used to set this net across and draw it at low water. We used to get skate, flat fish, and I got a lobster once. We kept on at this for three months. This pulled father right round and made a fresh man of him."

After a short spell of farm work Fred returned to the river and went after eels and flat fish. Sometimes he caught the eels by 'babbing' (using worms threaded on worsted yarn, which the eels caught their teeth in), at other times he used an eel gore (a device on a long handle of long sharp hooks placed fanwise and facing inwards, which was thrust down to where the eels might be lying). After the war he had a go at winkle gathering, and for four winters braved the cold going down to Wrabness. "I'd have two or three hours picking up winkles, then row back. Sometimes, coming back there would

Large punt guns mounted on Manningtree punts in the 1970s.

be a gale blowing down the river, and instead of an hour and a half, it would take me over three hours to row back, and I've had a job to get out of the boat at the finish – I've been so stiff and sore." It was not uncommon, he said, to have 90lb of eels squirming under the floorboards.

Fred stopped fishing in the early 1960s. He lived in Quay Street, close to the Stour Sailing Club premises, but then moved into one of the bungalows in Victoria Crescent. He used to stand by the boat compound with his hat secured to his collar by a piece of string in case the wind blew it off, and chat to passers-by about the old days. Fred Woollard had been a founder member of the present Stour Sailing Club in 1936.

Wildfowling continued at Manningtree until the 1980s. Several local people had punts - double-ended, flat-bottomed boats about 15ft. long that could be paddled close to flocks of duck at dusk by a man lying flat on the floor and using small paddles held in each hand over the side. The important thing was that the birds should notice no movement as the fowler approached so that the large punt gun, 8-10ft. long, could be fired into the flock. A punt gunner might kill 20 or more birds with one shot, though normally it was only a few.

One of the last to operate a punt gun at Manningtree was Peter Ainger, who built his own gun, took it to London on the train to have it proofed, and then used it on his punt during the autumn when the widgeon gathered on the estuary.

The Ainger family have lived in the area for over 200 years, and Peter Ainger was born in College Square, which is now College Court, in Manningtree. Peter, a part-time fisherman and wildfowler, also went after eels using pipes laid in the channel. The eel would hide in the pipe, and Peter would lift the pipe up at low water, holding both ends, then tipping the eel out into a bucket in his boat. Peter built his own smokehouse at his home in Colchester Road and used old pieces of oak salvaged from the demolition of Manningtree Church as fuel; these must have been the only eels to come out of a smokehouse filled with 17th-century smoke. "You could say Holy Smoke" as Peter used to say.

The punts today are not of the traditional type with their natural timbers, but of plywood, glue, and resin, which is much lighter. Locally built dobles, boats slightly bigger than

The beach in 1957 before the sea wall was built.

the punts and with a higher freeboard and transom sterns, were used for catching eels and other fish. They were made largely of deal, though the lower side planks were made from elm which stands up to wear better than the softer wood. Today the dobles are built of marine ply.

Before 1970 there was no sea wall, only a sandy beach where boats were pulled up out of the way of most tides. During big spring tides the water frequently came over the sand, flooded the fire station and crept up Quay Street and round the corner into South Street. One house that must have flooded occasionally was that which stood on what is now the Stour Sailing Club east boat and tent compound in front of the clubhouse. Members of the Porter family lived there at one time.

Spring tides, when the range of the tide is greatest, occur every fortnight, coming a day or two after a new or full moon. Tides vary, and tide tables give information regarding the expected height and time of high water. However, gales between the north-west and north-east, and other conditions, can add to these predictions. A northerly wind can push more water down the North Sea into the estuaries, and sometimes the tide seems to linger longer than expected.

Cold weather in December 2010 at Manningtree.

In January, 1953, a north-westerly gale, combined with low pressure and a high spring tide, built up a huge amount of water in the North Sea. It was during the cold night of Saturday the 31st that this surge of water hit the East Anglian coast, causing enormous damage and many deaths. At Manningtree the water lifted boats on to the road, and flooded its way up to the Market Cross.

During the winter of 1969-70 there were some very big spring tides which flooded over the sand, into the fire station, the wood yard, and round the corner into South Street. The weather was calm at the time; it could have been much worse had there been a high wind from the north or north-west. In the early 1970s the wall was built to prevent this happening, and following the scare of the 1978 high tides along the East Coast the sea wall was heightened even further and the road by the old Brooks maltings made higher to prevent water getting round the end of the wall.

One thing that is noticeable is how the mud has built up at Manningtree since the barrage was built at Cattawade around 1970/71, and the sluice gates on the southern arm of the river.

Boats left high and dry after the 1953 flood.

Above opposite: *A high spring tide, without any wind, in 1970. Note no sea wall yet built, and the firemen's exercise and hose drying tower, where the Stour Sailing Club boat compound is today.*

Below opposite: *The tide flooded along Quay Street towards Taylor and Butler's premises situated on both sides of the road. These high spring tides often flooded right up into South Street.*

57

The Manningtree Channel in 1963. A photograph looking east of the channel at Manningtree from the quay shows a low sloping side to the channel in 1963, whereas today there is a bank of mud. When the engineers were building they assured people that no increase in mud levels would take place.

Manningtree Regatta

Every year there is a regatta at Manningtree, with sailing races for dinghies, yachts, cruisers, and punts; and the mud sports, - when people run races through the soft mud at low tide or compete in the mud-splattered tug-o'-war. There has been a regatta here since the middle of the 19th century, when it was held during the second week of September. It must have stopped at some point, for there is a reference of Saturday 11th July, 1914, to "the third annual regatta held in the river Stour at Manningtree on Saturday, in fine weather, and in the presence of a large concourse of residents and visitors, who lined the riverside or floated contentedly in craft of varying description on the river. In Manningtree business was temporarily suspended. The main streets were gaily decorated, and shopkeepers and assistants flocked to the riverside".

The report goes on to say that "Mr. F. W. Horlock's sailing barge *Margaret* was moored in the channel and used by the committee. Mr. Edward Cant was starter;

Mr. G. K Cann, (Harwich), judge; and Messrs. J. Carter, (Harwich) and F. Dent, course stewards. The proceedings were enlivened by the Brantham Xylonite Works Silver Band (under conductor J. Naylor), who contributed an excellent programme of music which was much appreciated".

The Manningtree Channel in 2012.

The report, published in the local paper continues: "The regatta programme comprised eleven events, for which a handsome display of cash and other prizes were offered. There were 9 entries in the open boat race (25ft. limit), viz,.: *Bonito* 20ft. (Mr. F. Carter); *Slug*, 18ft. (Mr. F. W. Horlock); *May Queen*, 18ft. (the Rev. T. K. Norman); *Ena*, 15ft. (Mr. H. Quantrill); *Pixie*, 17ft. (Mr. A. L. Double); *Etona*, 18ft. (Mr. E. B. K. Norman); *Elnora*, 25ft. (Mr. W. B. Nichols); *Undine*, 21ft. (Messrs. L. and C. Horlock); and *Kelcie*, 17ft. 9in. (Mr. R. A. Horlock). The time allowance was 30 seconds to each foot, and the course from Coke Quay, Mistley, round mark boat at Stutton Ness, to Manningtree, round blue flag, to the Hook round mark, finishing at the Committee boat, channel side of all marks. The weather conditions were perfect when the 6 starters, viz: *Bonito, Ena, Slug, Pixie, May Queen*, and *Kelcie*, started. The *Bonito* early assumed the lead, which she maintained throughout, and finished an easy winner". Mr. Carter won, with Mr. Quantrill second and Mr. F. W. Horlock third.

Punt sailing at the 2011 regatta.

'Tubby' Baker sailing his punt in 1977. The punt, which he had for over fifty years, became rotten at the stern end, and was sawn off giving a rather unusual appearance of a Manningtree sailing punt.

Manningtree Regatta, 1914.

Amongst the races was an open boat race for maximum 15ft. craft, an open punt rowing race, a pair-oared skiff race for ladies, a men's skiff race, and the punt sailing race "which was splendidly contested". The entries in it were: "*Moorhen* (B Lucas), *Lion* (E. Ward), *Seagull* (W. Barnes), *Yaah* (C. Porter), *Banshee* (G. Porter), *Whippet* (E. Norman), *Golden Plover* (E. Lucas), *Snipe* (Jack Lucas), and *Rambler* (T. Lucas). Six started the 2 mile course, and their movements were watched with interest. It was a close race'. The result: '1st, Mr. Jack Lucas; 2nd Mr. Jas. Lucas; 3rd Mr. B. Lucas".

In the 1920s it was known as the water sports, and there were swimming races, a greasy pole to try your luck on, and the usual punt and rowing races. The Sailing Club was formed in 1936, and for an excellent history of the club and sailing, look at John Fairhall's *A History Of The First 70 Years of The Stour Sailing Club* published by the Club in 2006.

Manningtree punts are still raced in the regatta today. It is an art sailing these flat-bottomed craft, as there is no centreboard to grip the water and no rudder. They are sailed by oar alone, acting as both centreboard and rudder.

61

306

MANNINGTREE & DISTRICT

WATER SPORTS

Saturday, July 20th, 1935

President : W. H. H. BROOKS, Esq., J.P.

COMMITTEE :

Mr. K. J. Isaac (*Chairman*); Mr. T. W. Field (*Vice-Chairman*);
Dr. S. Bree, Dr. R. M. Erskine, Messrs. C. Arnold, E. Askew,
E. Greenwood, W. Ayton, A. E. Horlock, M. Horlock, E. Mower,
A. E. Norman, F. Peck, J. Pittock, Jnr., J. Read, W. R. Smith,
T. Temple, P. Whitehouse.

Hon. Treasurer : Mr. B. Young.

Hon. Secretary : Mr. J. F. Wright.

Judges : Mr. A. E. Horlock, Mr. J. Read (*Sailing Events*).
Dr. S. Bree (*Swimming Events*)

Starter : Mr. C. Arnold.

Timekeepers : H. L. Pattle and Dr. J. A. Hetherington.

Music and Announcements by the
Castaphone Sound System of Colchester
Commentator : MR. ALAN HORLOCK.

The Prizes will be distributed by Mrs. C. ARNOLD.

THE FIRST RACE (SAILING RACE BOATS NOT EXCEEDING
35FT.) WILL START FROM MISTLEY AT 2 P.M.

Save this Programme for the Lucky Number Prize.

PRICE 2D.

BC

1. **SAILING RACE** (O
   Time allowance 1 minu
   a channel course round
   line at Manningtree. D
   buoys to be left to starb
   3rd—15/- Special Prize
   Challenge Cup presente

2. **SAILING RACE** (O
   Time allowance ½ min
   Boat, channel side of a
   Start Boat, twice round
   Distance approximately
   2nd—10/- 3rd—5/- S

3. **SAILING RACE** (O
   Time allowance ½ min
   channel course to Hook
   leaving Beacon and Bal
   Mark Boat at New Mill
   at Manningtree. Dista
   buoys to be left to Starb
   and prize value 25/- 2r

4. **PUNT ROWING RA**
   Course about ½ mile. P
   START 3.15 p.m.

5. **PAIR OARED SKIF**
   Course about 1 mile. P
   allowed. Prizes value
   p.m.

6. **PUNT SAILING RA**
   Course—From Start Bo
   mark over mud opposi
   Distance approximately
   Starboard. 1st—Silver
   3rd—10/- START 4 p.

7. **PUNT ROWING RA**
   Course about ½ mile. P
   START 4.30 p.m.

1. Courses may be altered at
   weather conditions.
2. The Committee reserve to
3. Events, other than Open E
   Mistley, Lawford, Bradf
4. Four to start in any Even
   Second Prize given. N
5. The Council Quay will be
   and Competitors

NTS.

s not exceeding 35ft.

art at Coke Quay, Mistley, following
Red) Wrabness, return to finishing
imately 6½ miles. Marks boats and
Y 2/6. 1st Prize—30/-; 2nd—21/-;
uisers. 1st—25/- 2nd—15/- Silver
r. START at 2 p.m.

s not exceeding 12ft.

Course—From Manningtree Start
rk buoy in Thorn Reach, back to
and buoys to be left to Starboard.
TRY 2/6. Prizes value—1st—15/-
-

s not exceeding 16ft.

Course—Manningtree Start Boat,
thence a straight course over mud
(Black) on Starboard hand, round
channel course via Mistley to finish
ately 3¾ miles. Mark boats and
Y 2/6. 1st—Silver Challenge Cup
-10/- START 3.5 p.m.

). Entry 1/-

—10/- 2nd—7/6 3rd—4/-

en) (Open). Entry 1/-

eed 15ft. Light pleasure skiffs not
d—15/- 3rd—10/- START 3.45

Entry 1/-

se round Hook Buoy, thence round
dge to Start Boat. Twice round.
rk boats and buoys to be left to
up, Replica and 20/- 2nd—15/-

1/-

—15/- 2nd—10/- 3rd—5/-

SWIMMING AND OTHER EVENTS

1. **SCHOOLS RELAY RACE.** Teams of 4. 50 yards. Entry Free.
   Medals for winners and runners-up. START 3 p.m.

2. **GIRLS SWIMMING RACE.** Under 16. 100 yards. Entry Free.
   Prizes—1st—Silver Challenge Cup and Replica. 2nd—5/- 3rd—3/-. START 3.15 p.m.

3. **LADIES' SWIMMING RACE.** (Open). 100 yards. Entry Free.
   Prizes—1st—10/- 2nd—7/6 3rd—5/- START 3.30 p.m.

4. **YOUTHS' SWIMMING RACE.** Under 16. 100 yards. (Handicap). Entry Free.
   Prizes value—1st—7/6 2nd—5/- 3rd—3/- START 3.45 p.m.

5. **MEN'S SWIMMING RACE.** (Open). 440 yards. Entry 1/-
   Prizes value—1st—15/- 2nd—10/- 3rd—5/- START 4 p.m.

6. **LOCAL OLD BOYS' RELAY RACE.** Entry 1/- per team of 4.
   Medals for winners and runners-up. START 4.15 p.m.

7. **DIVING COMPETITION (Open).** Entry 6d. Free to children attending local schools.
   Prize value—1st—10/- 2nd—7/6 Special prize for children 2/6. START 4.30 p.m.

8. **NOVELTY RACE.** Mixed. (Open). 100 yards. Entry Free.
   Swim 50 yards in shorts, swim under spar, take off shorts, return over the spar to finishing line with shorts. Prizes value—1st—10/- 2nd—5/- START 4.45 p.m.

9. **COCKFIGHT (Open).** Entry Free.
   Prizes value—1st—10/- 2nd—5/- START 5 p.m.

10. **PRAM DINGHY RACE WITH SHOVELS.** (Open). Entry Free.
    Prizes value—1st—10/- 2nd—5/- START 5.15 p.m.

RULES AND REGULATIONS.

f the Committee according to the

right to accept or refuse any entry.

ed to the residents in Manningtree,
Cattawade and Little Bromley.

Prize given; Three to start or no
take more than three prizes in all.

d for members of the Committee

6. All objections must be made to the Hon. Sec. within an hour of the Event and be accompanied by a deposit of five shillings, which will be returned if the objection is sustained or not considered frivolous.

7. All objections will be considered by the Judge and Starters whose decision will be final.

8. Competitors enter all Competitions at their own risk.

9. Entries, accompanied by Entry Fees, should be made to the Hon. Sec. if possible, on or before July 18th, 1935.

ents are approximate and the Committee will endeavour to maintain the Time-table as far as possible.

Programme for the events of the Water Sports of 1935.
From the Stour Sailing Club collection.

Manningtree Regatta in 2007.

Around The Town – Manningtree 4

The main thoroughfare in Manningtree is the High Street, which used to form part of the main road from London to the port of Harwich; Samuel Pepys almost certainly came this way in the 17th century when he was clerk to the Navy Board and MP for Harwich. Now the main way to Harwich for most people in cars is the A120. Some years ago a restriction was put on the routing of heavy lorries through Manningtree, but occasionally they still appear. At the east end of the High Street, where the road narrows, rumbling traffic darkens rooms, sometimes takes drain pipes away, and shakes pictures crookedly, or even off the wall! The only large vehicles now using the High Street regularly are the buses between Colchester and Harwich.

Starting our tour at the Mistley end of the High Street, we can look out over the estuary towards the Suffolk shore and down-river towards Harwich. One house with a commanding view of the river is North House Gallery, formerly the home of

Removing the old tarmac ready for re-surfacing the road at Wherry Corner in 2011.

artist Blair Hughes-Stanton, a well-known painter and wood engraver. His daughter Penny has transformed her father's studio into a small but stylish gallery with regular exhibitions of contemporary artists' work. Actually this part of the town was formerly in Mistley, but now the boundary runs the other side of the houses here.

The sharp bend that takes us from the riverside towards the High Street is known as Wherry Corner, a reminder that a public house called The Wherry used to stand there. Wherry is a name for various kinds of small boat and also not-so-small vessels like those used on the Broadland rivers. Samuel Pepys used to take a wherry down the Thames when on Navy Board business or just out for pleasure. In this case the name may come from the sailing wherries that once operated a passenger service from Ipswich down to Harwich and very likely also worked the Stour. Indeed, in 1839 the landlord of The Wherry pub was John Moor, who owned a 'passage boat' called the *Sally* in which he carried passengers down to Harwich.

Blacksmith Walter Honeywood at work in the old forge in the 1930s.

The STOUR ESTUARY *is worth a visit and so is*

THE OLD FORGE CAFE

Facing the Stour

MANNINGTREE

TEAS, SNACKS, HOME-MADE CAKES, ICE CREAMS

Parties catered for   Phone 166   Also Open Sundays

Herbert Yeates advertisement of about 1950.

Opposite, on the corner of Quay Street is a cottage that was once, in the 1950s, Edward Sorrell's sweet shop. This was a time when there were something like thirty small shops in Manningtree itself, all somehow making a living, and we shall hear about these, and what they are now, as we travel through the town. The cottage has been a private home since the early 1960s.

Moving up from Wherry Corner we come to a row of cottages called English Terrace on the left, and ahead an arched entrance that once led into Alma Square. On the right of this arch was in the 1970s the surgery of Dr. White (and many years before that the Lifeboat Pub), and on the left in the 1930s the forge of Manningtree blacksmith Walter Honeywood. A picture survives showing him in his forge surrounded by blacksmithing paraphernalia. Cora Townes remembers when she was a little girl, how frightening it was to walk past the forge with the huge horses standing outside.

By the 1950s the forge had gone and Bert Yeates had turned the premises into a café and ice cream business. Bert had a fish round in the 1940s operating from an old Royal Mail van, but when he married in 1948 he moved into Forge Cottage and opened the Forge Café in the converted blacksmith's shop. Mrs. Yeates did the tea, home made cakes and snacks, and Bert ran the ice cream side of the business. In those days ice cream was a summer delight and was quite unknown in the winter, so Bert ran another sideline, second-hand furniture, during the winter months. Gradually the furniture side of the business took over and Bert Yeates needed bigger premises, so he moved to 17 South Street, which had extensive buildings at the back where he could store furniture.

Through the arch and on round the corner, we come to all that is left of Alma Square. The old houses, now gone, were one room down, one up, with a lean-to at the back for a kitchen. Families slept several to a room. In front of the houses there was a tap for all to use. Toilets were at the back, with a well that had a bucket that you lowered to get water for the toilet. Much of the square was demolished after it had been condemned as unfit for human habitation, and Brooks took over the site. When Brooks went, the area became part of the new housing estate at the end of Kiln Lane.

Manningtree High Street is a mixture of private houses, business premises and shops. Heading down the High Street, we pass the imposing front of the former doctors' premises of Dr. Sidney Bree, Dr. Beckett, and latterly Dr. John Kelly. A bit further on is Erskine House, named after another former Manningtree doctor, Dr. Robert Martley Erskine.

Opposite the opening to Stour Street is The Crown, a building with 16th-century origins. According to *Our Story, Lawford, Manningtree, and Mistley, the history of three parishes*, published in 1954, it was owned in 1704 by Ann Hewes and was once called The Rose and Crown. In the 1840s carriers were leaving three times a week for Colchester and twice a week for Ipswich from here. In the 1890s, it was known as The Crown Hotel. Today it is a Greene King pub and hotel run by Julie Bain. One can sit in the courtyard on a summer's evening while looking out over the river, or if the tide is out, at the boats lying at differing angles on the mud, but always an interesting view.

Joseph Glass remembers the place as the Rose and Crown:

> Mr. Tilman, the landlord of the Inn.
> Adroitly dealt in brandy, rum, and gin,-
> On customers he smiled – and was the man,

THE ROSE AND CROWN.

The next we find, was named the *Rose and Crown*,

An Inn it was that bore a fair renown ;

A blooming Rose the painted sign adorns,

With branching stem, and leaves, and pointed thorns—

Above the whole, a splendid Crown appears ;

As daily seen by all in former years.

To mark the score, and fill the flowing can;
He stirred the kitchen fire, when travellers came,
And bid them what they wanted quickly name;
A mutton chop, or steak, prepared quite nice,-
Just say, and they should have it in a trice.
Pronounced his porter good, and praised his ale;
No better in the town, he said, on sale.
The good opinions of his guests he'd win,
And all acknowledged 'twas a famous Inn.

69

Julie Bain, who took over the pub in 1992, and Bar Manager Simon Justice. 2011.

Today the Crown is a busy place where you can, according to the boards outside, enjoy a curry on a Monday and Tuesday; Wednesday is 'Pie and Pint Night'; Thursday is 'Fish and Chip Night'; or you can have a 'Two Course Meal With Glass of Wine - £10' while watching the 'Fantastic River Views'. For the 'Senior Citizen – 2 Course Meal £4.75'. This is a hotel as well, with plenty of accommodation and a 'Special Breakfast £3.75'. There is also a function room which can be booked free of charge.

Next door to the Crown is a shop that has had a variety of uses in recent years – an antique shop run by Ann Patterson, and before that a butcher's under several ownerships, Mr. Constable, A. E. & S. J. Sexton and Mr. Budd. At the time of writing it is a Body Sculpture Studio.

Passing the war memorial, listing 47 Manningtree men who fell in the First World War and seven who died in the second, we next come to Ike@47 – a café and shop run by Acorn Village, an organisation established in 1975 to provide a secure future for people who have learning disabilities. Acorn Village is housed in Mistley Hall, a Georgian country house set in six acres of land at Mistley, close to the Clacton Road. Here in Manningtree High Street they not only have the café and shop, but residences for up to six people. They have their own Care Manager, and although a branch of Acorn Village, they work independently. The house is the former Manningtree Rectory. Not much further along was at one time David Bones's bicycle and cycle repair shop at No. 41.

Opposite, where Nos. 42a, 42b, 42c, and 42d stand today, is the site of Manningtree Church. The original church, according to local historian Peter Gant, was not on this site but further up the hill, the exact location now lost in time. This older church was looked after by the Trinity Guild, who failed to keep it in good repair, so a petition was got up in 1610 for a new place of worship, resulting in the building of the Manningtree church in the High Street in 1616.

Dedicated to St. Michael and All Angels, the church seating capacity was enlarged three times between 1788 and 1839 by the addition of side galleries, a south aisle and a chancel. "No doubt the church could then accommodate a large proportion of the 1,250 parishioners, whose place of worship was elevated to the status of a parish church in 1840" wrote the rector John Morley in January 1967 when demolition was in progress. He goes on to say "Once the prosperity of the community had declined, the upkeep of the church building, now double its original size, became a real problem. But local people did their best and parish records clearly show that there is nothing of which to be ashamed. Although it was financially impossible to carry out a substantial re-construction envisaged in 1899, it was possible to make the best of the existing structure. The congregation did have a hard struggle to raise funds for fabric repairs, but they enabled the church to remain in use until 1964".

A detailed ecclesiastical report in 1922 said: "The parish church of St. Michael stands on the south of the main street. The north wall is of brick with some septaria and flint; the rest

71

*The church in
Manningtree in 1909.*

of the building is either of timber or is modern; the roofs are tiled. The church was built c1616 when it consisted of nave and North and South Aisles. The church has been much altered in modern times, most of the columns replaced, the Chancel added, and the South Aisle rebuilt and galleries inserted.

"The early 17th century hammer-beam roof is interesting. The Nave is of four bays with timber arcades formed of curved braces, springing from columns, which are now all of iron except the westermost on the North and West respond post, these being early 17th century octagonal or semi-octagonal posts of oak.

"The North Aisle (15½ft. wide) is mainly of early 17th century brick with some rubble. The windows and doorway are modern. The roofs of the Nave and North Aisle are of early 17th century date and of simple hammer beam type with curved braces to the hammer beams and collars; the shields at the end of the hammer beams are modern, except those in the North Aisle which are variously designed. The roofs are boarded below the rafters".

In 1964 it was found that massive hidden oak timbers were heavily decayed by the combined action of rot and death watch beetle. A report in the Essex County Standard stated that "The Queen is to be asked to approve the permanent closure. Experts think the condition of the church is so dangerous that it might

The interior of Manningtree Church from an old postcard.

collapse in a gale". The work of demolition was put in hand as a result of a Dangerous Structure Notice by the local authority and the withdrawal of cover by the insurance company.

All there is as a reminder that there was once a church here is part of the west wall and buttress next to the hairdressers, and a cast iron sign stating this was the site of the church. Since 1966 parishioners have used Mistley Church, which now serves both parishes, having been rededicated as St. Mary and St. Michael.

Joseph Glass, writing in 1855, remembered going to St. Michael's when he was young:

After demolition a space remained in the High Street throughout the 1970s.

Now five and fifty years have passed away,
Since we attended, on the Sabbath day;
And from a corner of the singing pew,
The members of the choir we had in view:
With clarionets, and flutes, and loud bassoon,
And violins, and one to guide the tune,
Who waved his hand, and sometimes looked askance,
While all were 'monished by his passing glance.

What music Joseph Glass conjures up in our heads today that was heard in Manningtree church in 1800! Among the treasures in the church was a painting of The Ascension by John Constable, presented to the church in 1822 by Edward Alston, a Manningtree brewer and Constable's cousin by marriage. When the church was demolished the painting was moved to Feering Church, and then sold. It is now on display in Dedham Church.

The memorials were moved to Mistley Church. Among them was one erected by the inhabitants in 1748 to Thomas Osmond, one of the Protestant martyrs put to death nearly three years earlier for refusing to attend Mass at Easter. The inscription reads:

To the pious Memory of Thomas Osmond a Fuller,
Who was burnt here at Manningtree
For the Protestant Religion.
Contrary to Humanity & the Mildness of ye Gospel,
In the Reign of Queen Mary.

He had neglected to receive Mass at Easter.
Whereupon he was brought before Bonner
Under a Strong Guard by the Earl of Oxford.
And upon his Answer to the Articles given him,
Was Condemn'd to the Flames,
And sent back to Suffer in the Place Where he had liv'd.

But the Council fearing a Tumult
Order'd the Lord Rich to arm the People of the Country
And see him executed.

He underwent Martyrdom with great Patience and
Constancy
On the 15th of June 1555.

But tho his Body was burnt to Ashes,
His Soul was translated
Into Heaven.

In the 1970s the space left by the demolition of
Manningtree Church still contained the tombstones of the
graveyard, but eventually these were moved to the cemetery
in Trinity Road, and new houses built on the church site.

On the other side of the road is the Lucca Restaurant,
an excellent eating place specialising in wood-fired oven
pizzas, and next door to that is a white-painted brick house
(No. 37) that was for a time the East Anglian Trustee Savings
Bank. Beyond that is the much older building occupied by
Townsends. This was formerly The Packet, which closed in
1914. "A house, two tenements, was built probably in the
15th century on an L shaped plan with the wings extending
towards the east and north. A wing was added on the north
of the east wing in the 17th century. Inside the building are
16th century moulded ceiling beams. The roof of the north
wing has an original king-post truss" says a 1922 report on
ancient buildings in Manningtree. The king-post truss was
done away with when alterations were made to the premises
a few years later.

In the 1937 Kelly's Directory it states that here was
the 'Ministry of Labour Branch Employment Office' at No.
33. In the 1950s this was managed by F.G. Townsend. The
Townsend family had bought the lease of Cullingford's
stationery shop, situated on the corner of South Street and
the High Street, in March, 1950, and ran that business until
1961. In that year they converted the old Labour Exchange
and the houses next door into what is now the shop run by
Michael Townsend and his wife Barbara. Before 1914 this
building had been The Packet Hotel, and before that The
Packet Inn.

Michael Townsend in his shop in August 2011.

Back to the south side of the High Street, there is Salon 42 Hair Shop run by Mr. and Mrs. Gee, who bought the business in 1981, when it was called Krystyna. This unusual name for a hairdresser's came from a former owner, Mrs. Erskine, a doctor's wife, who had a boat of the same name on the river. Elizabeth Gee was a hairdresser, and Robert Gee a marine engineer before they entered in the partnership to run Salon 42 - Elizabeth looking after the hairdressing side, and Robert seeing to the administrative and maintenance side of things.

Next to that is Dazzle, the dry-cleaning business; then No. 38, behind the frontage of which is a very old building with a cluster of six magnificent chimneys. This was also mentioned in the 1922 report as follows: 'Built probably in the 16th century and the remaining wing is of brick; the front block has been entirely rebuilt; there are 17th century additions on the South and East. The original wing has two windows of mullions, square heads and labels, all of brick; the six octagonal shafts with elaborately moulded bases. The outbuilding South of the house was built in the 15th century".

Inside Salon 42 Hair Shop, which is both a ladies and gents hairdressers.

Next to this is a Sue Ryder Care charity shop which was formerly a chemist's run by the Co-op, and before that by Mr. Winter. The Winter family must have been in business for something like over 150 years, for in 1839 Susannah Winter was a 'chymist and druggist' there. In one of Winter's old advertisements it is stated that the business was established in 1791. Harold Oxborrow remembered the shop in the early part of the 19th century when during the cold months of winter, there was a notice outside that said 'Hark The Herald Angels Sing, Winter's Pills Are Just The Thing; Peace on Earth and Mercy Mild, Two For a Woman, and One For a Child'.

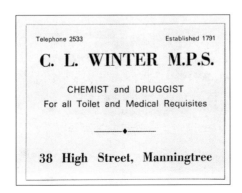

Telephone 2533   Established 1791

C. L. WINTER M.P.S.

CHEMIST and DRUGGIST
For all Toilet and Medical Requisites

———— ◆ ————

38 High Street, Manningtree

Winter's chemist shop advertisement.

77

Dragonflies, Tesco, Piper and Priem, and other shops as we look down the High Street towards the Market Cross.

Next comes Dragonflies – a gift shop – and then Tesco Express occupying premises that have been a village store for a long time. In the 1960s it was the International Stores, and in the 1970s James Newsagents. Continuing along we have Piper and Priem - where Stephen Priem will see to all your eye requests and problems; Out and About – men's and ladies country clothing – at No. 28; and the Whole Food Store at No. 26. In the past this had been a cycle shop and a newsagents.

This area seems always to have been shops. In the Church Magazine of October 1898 is the following:

> The local event of the past month has undoubtedly been the big fire, which broke out on the evening of September 2nd, and which was not extinguished till after an ugly gap had been made in the High Street. How it originated is not definitely known, but it was first discovered soon after 8 o'clock at the back of Mr. Newstead's grocery shop. The alarm was immediately given, and the local Volunteer Fire Brigade lost no time in getting to the spot, and fixing their hoses to the hydrants. Unfortunately, the water was at low pressure, the supply being practically useless for the extinction of the flames, which now assumed alarming proportions. A message was sent to the Waterworks at Mistley, and

more pressure obtained, but it was seen that the fire had got too great a hold to be put out entirely by local effort, and with local appliances, and therefore urgent telegrams were dispatched to Colchester, Parkeston, and Harwich for more help.

While this help was being sent, the fire was spreading furiously and soon Mr. Newstead's premises were engulfed in flames, causing commotion and excitement in the town and in the neighbourhood. The flames caught hold of adjacent shops, and at one time the outlook was decidedly grave, for appearance favoured the idea that the whole block of buildings would have to go. However our brigade worked untiringly, and when reinforcements arrived and got their improved machinery into working order, the united efforts soon began to tell.

As a precaution, and in order to save the Church, part of Mr. J. W. Downing's shop was pulled down, but this was unnecessary as things turned out, for the progress of the fire was stopped at the London and County Bank. In the other direction, the flames, besides demolishing Mr. Newstead's shop, made a complete wreck of Mrs. J. B. Winter's (whose husband was buried the previous Monday), and did considerable damage to Mr. H. J. Joyce's and Mr. G. Perks.

Some anxiety was felt for Mr. S. Hammonds across the road, but this house and shop were saved, thanks to the vigilance of the occupier and friends. The burnt-out trades people made immediate arrangements for carrying on their respective businesses in other parts of the town.

In the middle of the High Street is a building containing Togs Ladies Fashions and Togs Beauty Salon. Here also is the now empty shop facing east up the street that was for so many years Hammonds shoe shop.

Behind this building is The Lane, a narrow passage with a row of shops. The first one is Premiere Opticians. Here hangs a sign – 'Kodak Lens Vision Centre'. This indicates that this

This photograph of J. E. Cracknell's shop was taken about 1935.

company at one time supplied Kodak lenses for spectacles, but this is no longer the case. Now it is a place to have your eyes tested and order a new pair of glasses. In the 1930s this shop was quite different, yet another Kodak sign hung here, advertising 'All Kodak Supplies' meaning cameras, film, and accessories. Then it was run by J. E. Cracknell, and sold amongst other things wireless sets, picture frames, photographs, paraffin stoves, and tobacco and cigarettes. He also supplied the local paper with news stories, and advertised himself as photographer. When Queen Mary came to visit East Bergholt church the story goes he hid in the bushes and as she came out he approached her and asked if he could take a photograph. The people with her said no, but Queen Mary said he could, and asked him to send her a copy – which he did. The photograph made the Essex County Standard, the West Suffolk Gazette, and Eastern Counties Advertiser.

By 1937 Jack Cracknell's shop, which he had opened when he left the army, had gone, the directory listing the site as belonging to Edward Austin, who ran it as a drapery shop. It even sold books, and had a small library. Ann Ward remembers it as a shop 'that sold everything cheap – from dishcloths to knitting needles, from tea towels to toys'.

On the right is the same premises in 2012, with a view down The Lane.

Now we come to Chez Sue - Hair and Beauty salon; then at No. 2, 'Out In The Sticks', an antique shop selling old and new furniture and household bits and pieces. The final shop, at No. 1 The Lane, is 'The Hub' – a drop-in-centre for youngsters open Wednesdays 3.15pm to 5.15pm, and Thursdays 7.0pm to 9.0pm. A sign says 'The Hub is staffed by volunteers from local churches. We offer teenagers a comfortable, safe place to meet with their friends. In return we expect respect and consideration for each other, for the building, and its equipment, for our neighbours in The Lane'.

The Market Cross is where South Street crosses the High Street. On the corner in summer months people sit outside Café Rio, which adjoins Manningtree Delicatessen. On the other side of the road is R. Gwinnell & Sons, funeral directors; Robert Clubb & Co., accountants at 22a; Santander Agency Bank; Farthings second-hand furniture; and then the Library with its impressive colonnaded front of 1865. This building was erected as the Corn Exchange at a cost of £1,600. It was not a corn exchange for long, for it closed in 1875, and was then used as a public hall. In the 20th century it became a dance hall for a while, a furniture store, and then the Catholic Church. Now, as the area's library, it is busy with people from as far away as

Manningtree Library in 2011.

Dedham, East Bergholt, Bradfield and Wrabness. The Library houses the local museum, which contains a wealth of information about Manningtree and Mistley. Before the building of the Corn Exchange, as Joseph Glass records, farmers met and drank in The Packet, run by Mrs. Shead:

> And Harry Shead, her son, and eldest daughter,
> Then served the ale, and mixed the gin and water;
> Hollands and Brandy, too they served – and rum;
> And then secured the compensating sum.
> In front, on Thursdays, was a busy scene,
> Farmers from various parts, did there convene,
> To sell their stock, and all their store of grain,
> Pay their expenses and return again.
> Managed and regulated well within,
> Matters went smoothly at this noted Inn.

Back to the High Street north side opposite the library is a series of businesses and shops which have changed over the years.

Above opposite: The Market Cross with Rio Café customers in the foreground and the Manningtree Ox on the wall of the central building.

Below opposite: Manningtree High Street with the Public Hall on the right – now the library. Note the lamp post with 'Post Office' in the glass.

83

Ann Ward started working in the Aldis shop on Saturdays in 1959. She went full time as soon as she left school. This picture of Ann in the shop was taken in 2008.

There is the fairly new Bridal Shop called 'A Dream Come True', which is next to an old established business that closed down in 2011 – Aldis Fashions. John Wood, executor trustee, wrote in the Manningtree and Harwich Standard: "Our thanks go to all the customers of Aldis Fashions who have supported the shop over the years that it has traded.

"When my mother and father, May and Gordon Wood, purchased the property and business from the Miss Aldises in 1961, it had been a drapers shop for more than 100 years. Ann Ward has worked in the shop from leaving school and had been working for the Miss Aldises for two years before we took over.

"My mother May was ahead of her time; she had a brilliant business brain and she changed the drapers, haberdashers, and wool shop into a fashion and children's wear shop. May and her staff, Ann Ward, Gilly Andrews, Pat Gilbert, Ivy Dorman, and Iris Lay-Flurrie put in an enormous effort organising fashion shows in the local area.

"A new shop front was put in about 1965, giving the shop the ability to display its wares. May traded through some difficult years. Manningtree always seemed to be blessed and the business survived. The first major blow was losing the Ladybird Children's Wear range to Woolworths.

"May still had energy and continued running the business until her death in January 2004. Gordon died in August 2006. Susan, the surviving partner, suffered a stroke in March 2009.

"Latterly the growth in internet buying, TV selling channels, and catalogue sales, have all been difficult to compete with. They do not have the overheads that a High Street shop has and this, coupled with some changes in and around Manningtree, has not helped. Ann Ward's management has been crucial to the business since May's death. Maralyn Bambridge helped out initially until Janet Peck joined the team, and with her help, and sickness and holiday cover from Ann Rose, it has for me been a joy to be part of this long-standing business.

"Sadly for several years the business has just broken even. Latterly this has turned into loss and the decision to close has been made. The last trading day was April 2nd 2011. Thanks again for all our loyal customers".

In the early 1990s they enlarged and altered the shop, revealing that it was once a large family home going back to the 1740s, with a fireplace in the front room of the shop, two

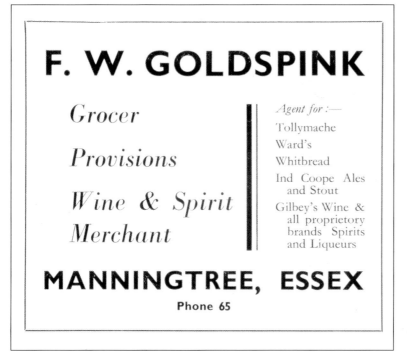

Goldspinks advertisement of about 1950.

staircases, and a well in the back room. The house has three storeys and a cellar, like many of the houses hereabouts.

Beside this now empty shop is Toys Plus selling cards, gifts, toys, and stationery. This was once Goldspinks, a high class grocery shop which also sold "spices, nutmeg, peppercorn, as well as brimstone and treacle" remembered Harold Oxborrow. "Every Friday night us boys used to have a spoonful of brimstone and treacle to keep us healthy". This shop was run by Frederick Wickham Goldspink.

Next, a door with brass plates which tells us here is the Manningtree Dental Practice and an osteopath, and beside that Spicer McColl, Estate Agents. Next door, in the 1970s, was Arnold and Son Ltd., 'For Fashions – Latest Styles in Ladies and Mens Wear' as a 1975 advertisement described the business. This was managed by the founder member of the Chamber of Trade, Len Fairclough. But that was many years ago.

The building has been done up during 2011 ready for two new shops. One is to be the restoration business and antique furniture shop of Mistley man Martin Hebblewhite. Martin does local conservation and painting work, with the shop being prepared as time allows. At the time of writing,

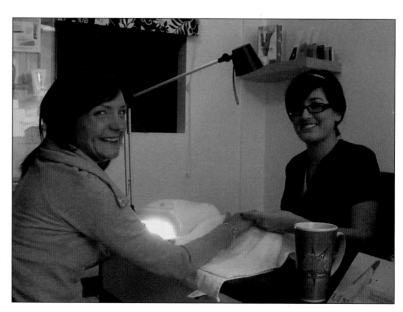

Gemma Garwood doing the nails of Jo Jenner.

in January 2012, the shop has not yet opened. Martin has worked on prestigious restoration and painting jobs all over the country. He has painted the door of 10 Downing Street; carried out restoration at Frogmore House in the grounds of Windsor Castle; done special decorative work at the Royal Pavilion in Brighton; painted and gilded 11th century stone ceiling bosses in Norwich Cathedral; re-lined and re-papered wall coverings in Prince Philip's bedroom; and restored and re-painted walls and decorative woodwork in the Queen's sitting room.

The shop next door is up and running, for it was opened in September 2011, and is called Divine, a Health and Beauty business run by Gemma Garwood.

Above the next shop, No. 15, it says Geo Paskell, Funeral Directors since 1837, and in the window a selection of gravestones. This is part of the Hunnaball Family Funeral Group. Sparling, Benham, and Brough are the solicitors next door at No. 13 High Street. This was formerly the solicitors run by Mr. Cox.

Opposite is the Post Office building, erected in 1939 on the site of Alston's brewery. A typical government building of

Martin Hebblewhite, painter and specialist in decorative restoration, at work on a house in Manningtree.

87

The White Hart in 1935, when they had a model hart (a male deer) above the entrance.

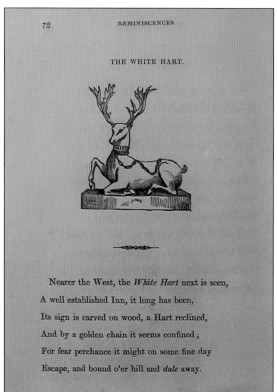

The White Hart from Joseph Glass's book of 1855.

its age, it has a scale that demonstrates the importance of the Post Office to a country town of modest size in those days. Before the Co-op at Fiveways incorporated the post office into their store, the counter was in this main building. Today it is the local sorting office, and only a small customer counter is retained for parcel pick-ups and PO Box numbers.

The Alstons, who ran the brewery, lived opposite in a house that was bought at auction by Dennis Howells, who about 1957 turned Wisteria House into a hardware and useful things shop. D. N. Howells and Sons, now owned and run by John and Neil, was established as a building firm in 1945. Besides the shop, they are 'Builders and Decorators; Plumbing and Heating Engineers; and Electrical Contractors'. Next door is the Acorn charity shop run by Acorn Village Trust, and then The White Hart, a pub once owned by the Alstons. As usual, Joseph Glass had something to say about the White Hart:

> Its sign is carved on wood, a hart reclined,
> And by a golden chain it seems confined;
> For fear perchance it might on some fine day
> Escape, and bound o'er hill and dale away.
> Mrs. Mallyon, as hostess we discern,
> Her husband could not manage the concern;
> With aptitude endeavoured to complete,
> To make both ends in fair proportion meet;
> While she herself attended at the bar.
> With her dependents, she would oft confer,
> Urge them to duty, and her plans explain,
> And when remiss, admonish them again.
> The Harwich coach, when passing through would stay,
> At this our Inn – change horses – then away;
> Collins and Paddle were the coachmen then,
> And both were careful and appropriate men.

A report of 1922 concerning the White Hart describes the Inn as being "built early in the 16th century. There is a long 17th century addition on the North, and an 18th century addition on the East. The upper story formerly projected on the South front, but has been underbuilt, and the whole refaced with brick. The upper story projects on the West side of part of the 17th century addition. Inside the building the former central hall has been divided up and part now forms a cartway; the hall has original moulded ceiling-beams and joists and two moulded wall-posts carved at the top with heads of a man and a woman. A room further East has also original moulded ceiling-joists." The White Hart itself, displayed outside above the entrance, quietly disappeared in recent years.

It is still possible to smell the baking of bread early in the morning in Manningtree. At 4am David Smith and Peter Kenny are up and about preparing the dough, and making a whole range of pastries, cakes and savouries. David Smith, with a family history in the bakery business in Leiston, Aldeburgh and Thorpe-le-Soken, owns De'aths in Manningtree High Street. David took over the business in January, 1985. Before then it was run by the De'ath family, and before that by Walter Peachey.

Peter Kenny joined the bakery when he was twelve, helping out on the van that at that time ran round Mistley, Manningtree and the villages of Lawford and Brantham, delivering bread and groceries from 8.30 in the morning until 6.00 in the evening. This village round ceased in the 1970s.

The bakery used to have a roaring fire and a traditional steam heated oven, but one December morning in the mid-1980s one of the steam pipes burst and the oven exploded, knocking out a wall. Now the bakery has modern electric ovens from which many shapes and types of bread emerge – all traditionally made on the premises without additives.

Loaves include bloomers, sandwich, long split tin, farmhouse, Danish and cobb, and there are new products such as ciabatta, foccacia, olive bread, and so on. Tanya, David's wife, who has been working for her husband since 1988, makes all the long-life food such as carrot cake and scones.

About 7.30 they begin drawing the bread out of the oven, for they want it fresh ready for the customers when the shop opens at 8.00. David prepares pastries and Peter continues to pull out the bread from the ovens on a traditional baker's peel.

In the mornings there are two people serving in the shop, though on Saturdays, the busiest day, this is increased to three. At one time there were seven shop assistants, but business has declined in Manningtree since the closure of the main post office, which affected many other shops in the High Street.

Once there were other bakers in Manningtree - Benjamin Rupert Edwards at 39 South Street; Ernest Smith at 17 South Street; and George King (later Brackpools) in Station Road. In Mistley there were only two bakers, Clatworthy and Smith in the High Street, and Walter Notley in Beckford Road. In 1848 Manningtree and Mistley had fourteen bakers between them.

On the other side of the road are the two big banks – Barclays, and NatWest – the latter on the site of a grocery shop run by Frank Robinson at No. 2 High Street. Opposite, on the corner with North Street is the fish and chip shop belonging to the Chilvers family. Barry Chilvers began peeling potatoes in his mother and fathers shop aged 13 in 1959, and soon took over the running of Manningtree Fish and Chip Shop. He is now retired, but like all retired people, he is busy – doing baby sitting for some of his thirteen grandchildren, and occasionally helping out in the shop. The shop is now run by John and Karen Chilvers.

There is a surprising array of food available. There are meat pies, scampi, chicken burgers, sausages, pickled eggs, onions – the list is endless. A portion of chips costs one pound, or you can have good old cod and chips for £3.70. There are soft drinks also, and 'skill' machines, as the money-in-the-slot

Telephone : 101

A. W. BRACKPOOL
MANNINGTREE

———

Grocer, Baker and Confectioner
Wedding and Birthday Cakes a speciality

Brackpools was not actually in Manningtree, but in Station Road, Lawford.

*Barry Chilvers still
helps out occasionally
in the Manningtree Fish
and Chip shop.*

amusement machines are called these days, where you can try
your luck with a 20p or 50p piece.

Further round the corner, into North Street there are
three small businesses – 'Paws Pet Food And Accessories';
'Reds Tattoo Parlour'; and 'Weddings and Proms'. In North
Street there are apartments converted in the 1970s from the
once extensive EDME maltings.

Anderson and Co, estate agents, are on the corner of North
Street and Station Road, followed closely by Manningtree
Grill and Pizza; Simply Thai; Hair@Number10; Rose Marie
Flowers By Toni; and The Skinners – formerly known as
The Skinners Arms. This name has a local significance; there
was a tannery behind the pub at one time, and for some years
afterwards cow horns were dug up in the garden. There was,
in the early years of the 19th century, a post mill behind the
Skinner's Arms. The windmill was actually just over the
boundary in Lawford, and was described in an advertisement
of 1810 as standing 'at the entrance to the market town of
Manningtree'. It seems likely to have been taken down in the
1820s, perhaps for re-erection on another site. It was by no
means uncommon for mills of this kind to be moved from

place to place. On the other hand many mills succumbed to fire; Daniels' Mill in Bradfield was burnt down in 1857, the accident being attributed to 'the overheated state of the machinery', the mill having been in constant use day and night. 'The engine from Manningtree was soon on the spot, but from the scarcity of water was of little avail' the Essex Standard tells us in its report of the disaster.

Opposite the Skinners' Arms there were once a number of buildings, the last of which disappeared in the clearance of this area in 1976. One shop that caused controversy was that of Percy Bloom. This business dealt in ironmongery, leather, handbags, watches, decorating materials etc. and also was at one time a harness maker. It had a history of 200 years trading, and latterly was run by the Sayers family. Several people wanted this building preserved, and at one point it was listed as a building of historic interest, but as time dragged on and the building became more dilapidated preservation became unrealistic.

The local paper said: 'With the disappearance of the shop, the area has lost a well-known landmark – or, in other opinions, a too-well-known eyesore. With the rubble removed and the memories of the conflicts erased, Lower Lawford

Station Road, looking towards Manningtree High Street about 1900. Percy Bloom's shop is the white gable building in the middle.

A 1954 advertisement for Percy Bloom's shop.

6th Generation

E. H. & A. M. SAYERS

Daughter aud Son-in-law of

Percy Bloom

Station Road - Manningtree

●

Will maintain the reputation built up over 200 years for—

QUALITY AND VALUE

Leather and Rubber soles, Fancy Leather Goods, Ironmongery, Household and Garden Requisites, Handbags & Watches

should be ready at last for some positive redevelopment'. Yes, this was in Lawford before the boundary changes of 1981.

A number of houses and flats known as Bendalls Court, named after the family who ran the nearby iron foundry, appeared on the site, and on the other side of Colchester Road, in Station Road, where there were also some small shops that were swept away, College Court was erected. A plaque in the wall by the zebra crossing explains that College Court and College Square take their name from an educational institution 'erected at the sole expense of Mrs. Cox of Lawford Place' in 1866. This plague, or stone block, was rescued by Lionel Randall from the demolition men – but it cost him £2.

Going along Colchester Road, as we approach the hill, on the right is Ironside Walk, on the site of the Lawford Iron Works. The ironworks, which was in Lawford before the boundary changes, was run by 'Joshua Robert Markwell Fitch (late O. Bendall & Son) engineer, iron and brass founder & manufacturer of agricultural implements, Lawford Iron Works. Telegrams "Fitch, Manningtree". Telephone 50' as the 1937 directory states.

The firm also specialised in deck machinery for sailing barges, which on some barges can still be seen with the name Fitch, Manningtree, picked out in white paint. The business employed many local people until its closure in 1971.

Before Mr. Fitch took over, the foundry was run by successive generations of the Bendall family, with a history going back at least to the 1830s. The 1834 milestone by the market place is by Bendall, informing us that London is 60 miles away. William White's 1848 directory lists Offwood Bendall as 'iron-founder and agricultural machine maker', and Ivan Sage in his *Lawford Life* says the company was formed in 1833 by David Bendall.

After the closure of the ironworks, the area was cleared and new buildings were put up to form what is now Ironside Walk. This complex for senior citizens incorporates Foundry Court Day Centre and is managed by Essex County Council. Here also is the Community Room run by Manningtree Town Council, for meetings and get-togethers, and when the time comes round, as a polling station.

Returning to the main road, next to The Skinners there is Boots Pharmacy and the 'East of England Co-operative Society Bereavement Services Centre'. Behind these is the

This building contains Ragmarsh Farm Shop, Entire Computers, and D.G. Financial Services.

Above opposite: *The Co-operative's Fiveways Store in August 2011.*

Below opposite: *Inside the busy Co-op on a Saturday morning.*

Phil Lorberg in Entire Computers.

Riverside Health Centre, where doctors John Hoskyns, Philip Bohannan, and Mary Kamanda can be consulted.

Now we come to Riverside Avenue East and a farmer's shop run by Richard Mitchell who sells produce from Ragmarsh Farm at Bradfield, and other sources. Now there is a butcher's shop in there as well. Next door is Entire Computers, where Phil Lorberg specialises in the repair, upgrade, and supply of computers; and upstairs D.G Financial Services Ltd. Beyond this, close to the estuary, is the Co-op car park and re-cycling area. At the far end is the Co-operative's Fiveways Stores, and beyond that Rose the builder's new yard and offices.

Back to Station Road, just by Lushington Road, is the corner-shop Stour View Stores run by Bhaskar and Varsha Patel. They took over what had been Oscar Tice's newsagent's shop in April 1984 and expanded the business considerably. Next door is the Manningtree and District St. John Ambulance headquarters.

It was in 1902 that Manningtree doctor Sidney Bree founded the St. John Ambulance unit in the town. The site in Station Road was used in the First World War as a transit base for soldiers marching to Harwich. The hut became the headquarters for the Manningtree Brigade, which in those days was just an ambulance division – except they had no ambulance, only getting about on foot or bicycle to render first aid. In the 1930s a nursing division was founded. Women ran the nursing part, making home visits to put people to bed etc., and relieving family members of responsibilities for a short while. They also attended public events. The men were out in the field, as it were, running the ambulance service. The two sets of volunteers did not train together.

After the Second World War, with the introduction of the National Health Service in 1948, home nursing became less needed, and the two components came together, the women training and working alongside the men. There were about twenty members at that time from Manningtree and the surrounding area. During the 1939-45 war they took part in training with the Civil Defence unit which was at Mistley Church Hall in New Road.

The primary job of the St. John Ambulance members is providing care in the community with volunteers trained to prevent injury and to save life. The Manningtree station was the first in Essex at the beginning of the 20th century, and only the third in the whole country. Dr. Bree was present at the 50th anniversary celebrations of the station in 1952.

Members continue to offer a service even in these days of rules and regulations that make running such an organisation complicated and expensive. Everyone sees the members on duty at big public attractions, such as the Tendring Show, but few realise that the St. John Ambulance members are all volunteers, and that money has to be raised to keep the organisation going and to maintain the special ambulance and keep it up to date. This is housed within the building in Station Road, even though it is technically on loan from the Essex headquarters in Chelmsford. An ambulance is required by law at big public events.

When it became necessary to replace the wooden transit hut that had served the organisation for at least seventy years they had to find £80,000. With the help of grants from Essex County Council, the Stour Valley Fund Raisers, and the National Lottery, and much hard work by members and friends, the new building was opened in October, 1996. The premises include offices, a large training and lecture room, store rooms, kitchen and toilets. Today the hall is occasionally used for other public events.

On the north side of Station Road, half in Manningtree and half in Lawford, stood a mixture of buildings, the main ones used until 2006 by Railex, a firm making metal office furniture, high density compact shelving, and mobile storage systems. On 7th October 2005 the Manningtree and Harwich Standard reported that: "After more than 40 years Railex, the filing system manufacturer, is leaving the town. Employees at the Station Road company were told on Wednesday morning and, in a statement issued afterwards, chairman Howard Wilson said: 'We have for sometime now, had a very interested party wanting to acquire the site in Manningtree. We have today sold

Lushington Road and the corner shop Stour View Stores.

the site to them'". The report mentions new equipment and a new location for the company, and goes on: 'This investment will increase our efficiency and contribute to making us more cost-effective in support of our efforts to achieve growth and success' said Mr. Wilson. 'All employees will be fully involved in discussions as to how these plans affect them. These measures have been taken to safeguard the future of the company and to bring us back into profitability'. Formerly known as Elite, the company was founded in Colchester by Harold Mitchell, and moved to Manningtree in 1962. In 1985 it was extended by 5000sq.ft.; in 1987 the neighbouring Coca-Cola depot and nearby a derelict bungalow was taken over; and the following year the premises were increased by a further 6,500sq.ft.".

Tesco had acquired the site, and on 26th July 2011 Tendring Council finally gave the go-ahead for the new store after many meetings and much controversy between those that wanted a Tesco in the area and those that did not.

Before the Railex factory came here, there was a small lane of houses called Marsh Row, which, according to the late Lionel Randall, used to flood at very high tides. Close to these

Bhaskar Patel in his shop on the corner of Lushington Road.

houses was a plot of land used by the travelling fairs which were popular at one time.

Next to the St. John Ambulance station on the south side of Station Road are Leander Cottages, three mock-Jacobean dwellings built in 1925. Originally these almshouses were for widows or unmarried daughters of fishermen or sailors, who had to be teetotallers and evangelical Protestants. The almshouses were the result of a bequest from Sophia Leander, of New Beckenham in Kent. The Isabella Sophia Leander Trust was set up in memory of her father, mother, and a cousin. The Trust, actually known as the Moat House Bequest, got a £14,500 lottery grant in 2002 to provide wheelchair access ramps to each cottage and new pathways around the terrace. Why Sophia Leander picked Manningtree as a place for these almshouses remains a mystery.

After three more houses comes the sign 'Welcome to Lawford'. Here Manningtree officially ends. It is worth mentioning before we leave this part of the town, that many people at one time walked along this road to the cinema, which stood just past the west end of Victoria Crescent.

The Railex factory in 2006, now to be the site of a new Tesco store. Note the Manningtree sign marking the boundary with Lawford, in the middle if the picture.

It was the last building before open countryside; this was well before the Westfields estate was built. The Cinema, as it was known at the time, was owned by the Tozer and Linsell Circuit, a London company with cinemas in Braintree, Halstead, and Saffron Walden. It was built as a silent cinema, and a poster of 1926 advertises Olive Borden and Ralph Graves in '*The Country Beyond* – The story of a backwoods girl who brought her feet to Broadway – and Broadway to her feet', along with the drama '*Call Of The Road*'; the comedy '*Flaming Romance*'; and a '*Gazette*' – a newsreel. This programme was for Monday, Tuesday and Wednesday. The next three days had Betty Blythe and Herbert Langley in *Chu Chin Chow*, a film described as with 'gorgeous settings, and excellent acting'. The manager of The Cinema was Sidney Holt, and the poster was printed by 'Cullingford and Co., Ltd,. Printers, Colchester and Manningtree'.

Although actually in Lawford, The Cinema is listed in the *Kinematograph Year Book* of 1928 as in Manningtree, which, it states, had a population of 870. In 1956, when the cinema was owned by an Ipswich company, Owen Cooper Theatres, it was known as The Plaza, and advertised the programme as 'Continuous from 5.30pm.' Many people remember going to this cinema, and tell stories of how the lower stalls used to flood after heavy rain, and patrons had to move back a row at

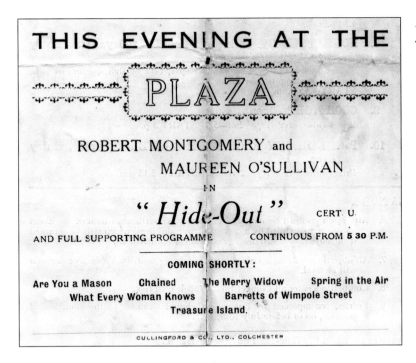

An advertisement of July 20th 1935.

The old cinema building in the 1970s, just before demolition.

a time to keep their feet dry, and that the screen dialogue was difficult to hear when the rain clattered loudly on the tin roof.

In 1959 Cinemascope was installed. This was rather late in coming, as this widescreen system using ordinary film with the image 'squeezed' onto the tiny frames of picture by the use of an anamorphic lens, was introduced in 1953. For independent and small cinemas where the cost of the lenses proved prohibitive at first, special 35mm prints of cinemascope productions were made, losing a little of each side of the picture. The Cinema at Manningtree would have hired these prints until 1959 when it could afford to install the new screen necessary and the anamorphic lenses. The first cinemascope film to be shown at The Plaza, as the cinema was known at the time, was "No Time To Die" featuring Victor Mature and Leo Genn on August 3rd, 1959.

The cinema closed in the 1960s, and the building remained in place being used as a store for the company that built Westfields. It was quickly demolished in the 1970s, when houses were to be erected on the site.

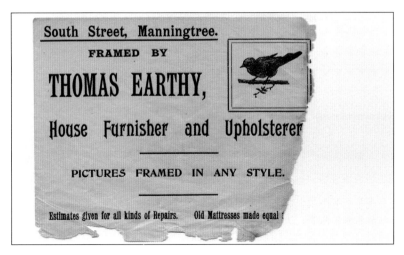

South Street, Manningtree.

FRAMED BY

THOMAS EARTHY,

House Furnisher and Upholsterer

PICTURES FRAMED IN ANY STYLE.

Estimates given for all kinds of Repairs. Old Mattresses made equal

Going Even Further   5

Back in the centre of Manningtree, standing at the Market Cross we can look both ways along the High Street. It once had two names, West Street going west, and East Street. The Manningtree Market charter dates back to 1238, the original market day being on a Monday. During the Middle Ages, every year at the fair the town roasted a whole ox, and the Manningtree ox became known throughout the country. It was even immortalised in Shakespeare's Henry IV Part I where Falstaff is referred to as 'that roasted Manningtree ox with the pudding in his belly'. During the Manningtree Festival in May, 2000, the actor Warren Mitchell, who played Alf Garnett in the television series 'Till Death Us Do Part', unveiled a metal sculpture by Colin Wilkin overlooking the Old Market Cross. The sculpture was sponsored by the Rotary Club of Manningtree Stour Valley. According to Pigot and Company's *Commercial Directory*, published in 1839, 'the market is on a Thursday, and a fair for toys and pleasure on the Friday in Whitsun week'. Here at the Market Cross was once a shed, with a tiled pitched roof, containing the Manningtree fire engine. Where the roof abutted onto the big brick building the lines of the eaves can still be seen.

The name Earthy seems to pop up quite a lot in records. There was an Earthy in Mistley described as a candle maker in the 1870s. James Earthy was a furniture dealer and beer retailer in South Street; Thomas Earthy is listed as a shopkeeper in 1890; and in 1899 as a bill poster as well. The last directory to mention him is Kelly's in 1937 which says 'Thomas Earthy and Son, bill posters, 32 South Street'.
This un-dated scrap of paper found in the back of a picture frame lists Thomas Earthy as 'house furnisher, upholsterer, and old mattresses made equal to new'.

Minar Miah and some of his staff of the Mogul restaurant.

The ancient building now known as The Mogul has in recent times been an antique shop and a coffee shop, but now it is a well-known Bangladeshi restaurant run by Minar Miah along with his nephew, the celebrated chef, Sunu Miah. Minar ran a similar restaurant in Barnet before he came to Manningtree in 1991. Sunu, who specialises in Bangladeshi and Indian curries, has won many awards for his skills at preparing food.

Locally based TV stars regularly eat at the Mogul, as can be seen from the Mogul's press cuttings book, but the quality of the food is known well beyond Manningtree. In 1998 the Mogul sent one of its dishes to London by helicopter to feed a visiting pop group, and a year later Hugh Hefner ordered a chicken tikka masala to eat at his home in Los Angeles! Minar has more recently been talking about the Mogul and its food on BBC Radio – so the fame of the restaurant continues to spread.

The Mogul occupies a building that is probably early 15th century, but is said to have been rebuilt in the 16th century. It has a cellar with a series of brick niches with four-centred heads.

Opposite, roughly where Café Rio now stands, was Sadler's shoe repair shop before it moved to the present site in Stour Street, on the site of the former Kings Head public house which closed in 1915.

On the corner of South Street and the High Street is the funeral directors R. Gwinnell and Son (these premises were formerly J. Van Der Gryn's fruit, florist, and greengrocer shop, and before that a Co-op shop selling clothes and shoes) and on the other a shop that has had a variety of owners and uses over the years, including in the 1950s and 1960s Cullingford's, the stationers. No business seems to stay there long, and the last one, Manningtree Anglers Ltd. - with 'Maggots now in stock', is gone – having closed at the end of September 2011. Over the road is V & M Racing Ltd, a licensed Betting Office, formerly a bookshop, and before that a grocers and confectionery shop run by Bertie Bullock, who grew his tomatoes and vegetables on the allotments at the back of Stour Street. Next door is a barber's shop, always busy, always full.

At one time, in the 1930s, there were three barbers in Manningtree – Frederick Worth at 26 High Street, Harold Oxborrow in Station Road, and Frederick Mortlock at 21 High Street. Mistley had just the one, Reginald Stocker. There were two ladies' hairdressers in Manningtree, Dorothy Fryatt at 18 South Street and Eileen Worth in the High Street.

The present barber's in South Street is run by Matthew Cackett. People come from miles around to have their hair cut in Manningtree – Matthew's is one of the few small-town

J. Van Der Gryn's shop was on the corner of South Street and the High Street, where Gwinnell's now is.

107

Mark James Morsley with Ann Morsley and Claire Bannister.

men's hairdressers left, and there is always a number of people waiting to have their hair cut inside, and early in the morning just before opening time, a queue outside on the road.

Next to this is a house with a bay window, once a sweet shop run by Mrs. Florence Mary Chenery. Then comes two offices - Mark J Morsley & Associates Ltd, Independent Financial Advisers, Mortgage & Insurance Brokers, and MJM Estates, an estate agency. Both are part of the same organisation owned and run by local businessman Mark James Morsley. Mark started his career in financial services with the Prudential in 1990. He joined Allied Dunbar in 1995 and in 1996 he became an Independent Financial Adviser. He started his core business, MJM Financial Services Ltd, from his spare room in 1999 and moved into 14 South Street in February 2000. The company changed its name in 2010 still providing a service to the town as it has done for 11 years. Mark is also a Manningtree Town Councillor.

These premises were once the home of an ironmongery and men's working clothes shop called Calver and Arnold. Mr. Calver was responsible for the clothes side of the business, and Reginald Arnold looked after the hardware and electrical goods.

South Street in 2011, with the estuary and Brantham beyond.

After crossing Stour Street we come to Exchange House, formerly the home of Harwich Radio and Cycle Supplies. The shop was closed in 2005 on the death of John Honeywood, the manager. Now the premises is an Osteopathic Clinic. On the opposite side of the road is No.17, The Old Corner House, once the home of Bert Yeates, who had an estate agency business, H.E. Yeates and Co. Before that it was the baker's E.W. Smith, run by J. Spilling.

Looking down South Street in the 1950s.

109

Bert Yeates made a living dealing with second-hand furniture, and letting chalet bungalows in Jaywick. Gradually people began asking him to find them permanent housing, so he became a qualified estate agent and started H.E. Yeates and Company, Estate Agents, in the early 1960s.

In January, 1980, he sold the business to John Anderson and Norman Cory. They bought No. 21 South Street and began doing up the premises. Previously No. 21 had been an opticians, and when John and Norman opened the new estate agency people kept coming in asking for their eyes to be tested. Anderson and Co. have since moved to the corner of North Street and Station Road.

A bit further up on the left-hand side is No. 23, which was at one time a small tobacconist's shop run by Mr. Phillip Cole, who also had a clock and watch repair business on the premises. Mr. Cole retired in 1957, and the repair side ceased. The tobacco shop was taken over by E. and M. Drover, who introduced a wholesale service alongside the shop, supplying many public houses, clubs, and shops in the area. On their retirement in 1977 the business closed and the property sold.

Boys in South Street in 1957.

The New Dragon House selling Chinese Food To Take Away is on the right, and then the Red Lion public house. Opposite is the old Manningtree Mechanics' Institute building, mentioned by Joseph Glass in his reminiscences:

> Proceeding on our way with free good will,
> We ascend what formerly was Wormwood hill;
> When soon upon the left hand side is seen,
> An old, antiquated pile, we ween.
> Now this is the Mechanics' Institute,
> And is undoubtedly the pleasing fruit
> Produced by good and well matured designs,
> Of several philanthropic, active minds.
> Such minds indeed, as these, deserve renown,
> May they exist in every British town,
> As in this case, produced ample fruit,
> A good, and well established Institute.

This was built in the 1840s, and served to bring news of the latest scientific advances to the working people (the mechanics) of the town. Now known as the Masonic Hall, the building has been used for a variety of functions, at one time serving as a polling station in election years.

Girls in South Street in 1957.

111

The Green, with the Red Lion on the right in 2011.

Now we come to The Green, a small open space where it has been said Matthew Hopkins carried out his bizarre and brutal rituals, though there is no actual evidence for anything having happened here. Behind No.48 is a splendid building faced in white brick which was once the Independent Meeting House, opened in 1823. It has had several names over the years – Independent Chapel, Congregational Chapel and Round Chapel. In 1929 it became the home of the Manningtree and Mistley and District Branch of the British Legion. It was sold in 1975, and is now in private hands and known locally as Robin's Shed.

Looking towards York Street from The Green. The old gasworks chimney is in the background.

The Congregational Chapel in 1906, now known as Robin's Shed.

On the left now is York Street, fronted by a row of small terrace cottages. Here once was the showroom of Eastern Electricity, where people paid their electricity bills and looked at new cookers. Electricity was first supplied by the Colchester Corporation electricity department in the mid-1930s, and the former showroom, now York House, still bears the Colchester Borough arms although the old showroom window has long been bricked up.

If we walk down York Street we come to the corner where Oxford Road goes up to the right. Here, on the other side, was the site of the old works of the Manningtree and Mistley Gas Company. Every town once had its own gasworks, making gas from coal, and producing as by-products bitumen and coke. C. Stone and Son, the coal merchants in Norman Road, had a licence to deliver coke from the gasworks to their main customers. Some locals however used to queue up to get rough coke, which burned easily, to take away in any kind of cart or receptacle they could muster.

Manningtree gasworks was built in 1840 at a cost of £1,700, and the gas was available as far away as Manningtree Station. In 1890 gas lamps were put up along The Walls and in the streets of Mistley. The gas street lamps were not lit for two days before and two days after full moon, people being expected to see their way around by moonlight.

113

Coal was brought from the railway station at Mistley to the gasworks to be put into the retort to make the coal gas, which everyone had until North Sea gas came into the pipes in the late 1960s. By the gasworks site is a reminder it was here, as the path straight ahead is called Gasfield, and part of the wall on the north side is built of clinker from the works. In Carlyon Hughes's *The History of Harwich Harbour* is the following entry of 1936: "A complaint was received from a landowner at Stutton as to alleged pollution of the waters of the Stour, and Dr. W.G.C. Baldwin was asked to investigate the matter. He found no source of pollution on the North side of the river, but found that large quantities of poisonous gas liquor were being discharged from a pipe belonging to the Manningtree Gas Company. Notice was given to the Company to remove the pipe".

Going up Oxford Road we pass Regent Street on our right, where at No. 17 Thomas Young had a small shop. There are

Oxford Road in 2011.

attractive cottages on the Mistley side of Oxford Road, houses
that are old enough to have attracted Joseph Glass's attention:

> We see upon the left in order stands,
> The numerous works of Mr. Monteith's hands,
> For Oxford Road 'tis known – and Regent Street,
> Were first designed by him and made complete!
> It seemed to us in toil, he took such pleasure,
> We thought, indeed, it was his chiefest treasure.

James Monteith, whose numerous works are referred to
by Glass, is listed in Pigot's directory of 1839 as a gentleman,
and in the 1841 census we find him living in Oxford Road and
described as 'ind' – meaning a person of independent means.
It has been suggested he lived at the far end, where Oxford
Road meets New Road, possibly in Oxford House which
looks down Oxford Road, but I am surmising that. James
Monteith, who was born in London in 1778, and Joseph Glass
may well have been close friends. It looks as though Monteith
must have built workmen's cottages and some slightly larger
houses on land that he owned, thus forming Oxford Road and
Regent Street. His money probably came from his coal and
salt business on Manningtree Quay. It is recorded that in 1826
the ship *Oeconmey* carrying coal from Newcastle called at
Manningtree to deliver coal to Mr. Monteith.

Monteith's coal and salt business was taken over in
1829 by William Shansfield who was listed in 1823 as a
'grocer, linen draper, tallow chandler & melter'. In March
1829 Shansfield stated "Having engaged that old established
concern, The Salt Office and Coal Yard, late in the occupation
of Mr. James Monteith, begs to inform the friends of his
predecessor and the public in general that he intends keeping
a large stock of fine coarse salt, and will have it in his power
to charge the trade on such moderate terms, for ready money
only, and will he trusts ensure him their countenance and
support. W. S. has by him a quantity of agricultural salt. The
yard will regularly be supported with coals of the best quality,
at the general price".

William Pinkney, headmaster of the Wesley School, from a photograph taken in 1927.

In the next listing, Pigot & Co.'s Directory of 1832, William Shansfield is listed in two places. Under:

Coal Merchants.
Shansfield, William (and salt works) Manningtree.

Under Grocers and Drapers
Shansfield, William (and tallow chandler) Manningtree.

In 1848 Shansfield is listed as 'tallow, chandler & salt and coal merchant' in the High Street, Manningtree. After that, we hear no more of him. James Monteith was still living in Oxford Road in 1851 - aged 73, according to the census of that year.

Going back to our journey along Oxford Road, the Manifest Theatre set back on the right occupies the old Wesley School, opened in 1854. From 1922 to 1947, William Walter Pinkney, a member of an old Mistley family, was headmaster here. He took an interest in all things local, and was master of Mistley Methodist Choir; Honorary Captain of the Boy's Brigade; a physical training examiner; lecturer to the Boy's Club and the L.C.C. Home at Brunswick House. He was also a committee member for the constructing of the new open-air war memorial swimming pool built on the foreshore at Mistley in 1931.

The Wesley School, and St. Michael's School in Trinity Road, merged in 1976 to become Manningtree Primary, with Mrs. Reynolds as headmistress of both, though the schools stayed in their respective buildings. Then on 21st July 1978, when the new school at Highfields, overlooking the town, was ready, everyone moved in. Infants from the Wesley and the older juniors from St. Michael's were given TSB plastic carrier bags to put their books and belongings in, and then, led by Mrs. Reynolds, and a band playing, they marched to their new home.

One pupil from St. Michael's remembered the day. "At about 1.15pm we walked out to the top of Mill Hill and the Royal Staffordshire Regiment's Band came over the bridge with the children from the old Wesley School following. They went down the hill and we followed, all carrying our TSB plastic bags with our books in. Two ladies carried a banner to show everybody that we were moving to our new school. Left - into Colchester Road and up through masses of parents who joined in behind us. Along the road by the new Sports Hall and round to the back of our new school and into the playground.

"We listened to the band for about twenty minutes and then there was a speech from Mr. Cooper who was opening the school. He then let off balloons with our names on and some of them burst in the orchard, and one landed on the roof of the school, but most of them sailed away.

"Next into our respective classrooms and we had some food and drink. The food was all laid out in the hall for the visitors who included many old pupils, head teachers and one lady who taught at the school before the First World War. We said some prayers and then went home to our parents".

So the Wesleyan Day School, or as it was known in more recent times, the Wesley School in Oxford Road, was no more – but another future lay ahead for the building. It was in

The children from the Wesley School walking up South Hill on their way to the new school at Highfields on 21ˢᵗ July 1978.

117

1977 that a group of people, including Bruce Emeny, Dennis Murfitt, Val Taylor, and Viv Wheatley, formed The Manifest Theatre Group. There were sixteen interested people who each put £1 in to get it off the ground. The first production was in Robin's Shed in May 1979. After a lot of fund raising, the group was able to acquire its own building, the old Wesley School, in October 1985, and name it The Manifest Theatre. And now in the converted classrooms, actors act and films are shown, while members of the audience sit in genuine theatre tip-up seats.

Continuing up Oxford Road, Norman Road is on the left, and then we cross the railway line and the Manningtree boundary and enter Mistley, emerging near the former Waggon and Horses.

Back now to York Road and the corner of South Street and continue on up South Hill, as it used to be known.

On the left is a house with large shop-like windows which was once the Gas Showroom, at 39 South Street. On the other side of the road, at number 58, was a small family grocery shop run by Sammy Sargent, who also sold toys, stationery, seeds, fertilisers, cups and saucers, and Lyons Ice Cream. It is said that the schoolchildren from the Wesley and St. Michaels schools spent their pocket money in here buying sweets.

Opposite is Regent Street, part of the expansion of the area in the 19th century by Mr. Monteith. Further up we come to the large and imposing Methodist Church, built in 1807 and lauded by our friend Joseph Glass:

> And now endowed with a progressing mind,
> We further on, another structure find;
> On elevated ground, it firmly stands,
> And as we know, upraised, by Wesleyan hands.
> And like our church has been extended;
> Convenience, and appearance, was intended.
> In this we find they have succeeded well,
> As numerous friends, and neighbours, all can tell.

With its white-brick pedimented frontage surmounted by a cupola the Methodist Church occupies a prominent position in the townscape. The wear on the stones leading up to the main door shows that it has been well used over the past 200 years.

John Wesley visited the area in 1785 and found at Mistley Thorn 'a lively society and one of the most elegant congregations I had seen for many years'. Apparently this 'society' had been founded by a shipwright from Deptford Dockyard who had been sent down to oversee the building of some warships in the Mistley shipyard and had read sermons to little gatherings in his house of a Sunday evening.

Beside the church is the church hall, opened in 1935. It is now the Methodist Community Hall, much enlarged and comfortable. It is used for meetings, talks, and the annual art exhibition. It is also the place where the Manningtree Society; the Chess Club; the Manningtree History Society; the Co-op

Opposite: Members of the cast of the October 2011 production of Daphne Du Maurier's Rebecca.
The players, from left to right are: Frith – Albert Horn; William Tabb – Gordon Prior; Giles Lacy – Mike Johansen; Beatrice Lacy – Jennie Horn; Frank Crawley – Lester Pearse; Mrs. De Winter – Jazmine Chandler; Maxim de Winter - Nigel Lister; Mrs. Danvers – Susanne Harknett; Jack Favell – Adam Duarte-Dias; Colonel Julyan – Alan Wheeler; Robert – Robert Duarte-Dias. At the front is the director, John Roberts.

119

Women's Guild; the Stour Choral Society, and others, meet on a regular basis.

Looking at the building from the road, what is intriguing is the stone blocks set in the wall at the front from corner to corner under the windows. Each block is numbered in Roman numerals I-XIV (1-14). What were these figures for? The answer lies inside the Hall.

There is a plaque on the wall stating that
'The Stones of the New Hall Were Laid on Oct 10th 1934
by:

I	Mrs. Thomas Currey.	IX.	Miss. Pamela Tice.
II	Mr. J. W. Long Senr.	X.	Mr. Cecil Bloyce.
III	Mr. Harry Mead.	XI.	Mrs. A. Manning.
IV	Rev. Maurice Poole.	XII.	Mrs. E. E. Milk.
V	Mr. William Pittock.	XIII.	Mrs. John Currey.
VI	Mr. Thomas Crisp.	XIV.	Mr. Edward J. Keeble.
VII	Mr. Harry Holland.		Doors Were Opened on Jan 16th 1935
VIII	Mrs. F. G. Cook.		by Mrs. W. Hilton Brooks
			& Mrs. J. Harman'.

The answers to the numbers on the stone blocks on the outside of the 1935 Methodist Church Hall.

Ahead of us is Grove House. To the left of this building was the office of Parsons the building contractors, and even now over the bricked up door is a relic of this company which closed in the 1980s – a glass panel with 'Parsons' still visible. William Parsons was an undertaker, carpenter, joiner, and monumental mason; while the company, Parsons and Son, founded in 1815, were 'sanitary engineers and house decorators'.

William Parsons is recorded in 1848 as a glazier and painter in 'South Hill', while William Parsons junior was trading at Mistley at that time under the heading in the directory of 'Plumbers, Glaziers, and Painters'. According to one of their advertisements published in 1937 Parsons and Son were sanitary engineers, house decorators and plumbers, and offered 'funerals completely furnished'. They were also regional agents and installers for Aga cookers. They even installed one in a boat! At that time William Parsons was running the firm, but later his son, Newman Charles Parsons, took charge. On his death in 1963 managers were brought in, but the firm ceased trading in 1985. The company had an extensive yard at the back, which is now the site of a small housing development called, appropriately, Parsons Yard.

South Street continues on, even though the road markings give the impression that you are entering another road. In fact the top of Brook Street terminates on the right at the junction with South Street, which continues up past cottages on the left, and Alexandra House (once a pub) on the right, to the railway bridge where we come into Trinity Road, which is in Mistley. Trinity Road was named after the Trinity Guild which supported the original Manningtree Chapel of Ease to Mistley Church, prior to the new church being provided in the High Street in 1616. In the wall just over the bridge on the left is a King Edward VII letter box – red and waiting.

Close by here was Trinity Farm, which belonged to Brooks, the animal feed firm. They had a dairy, prize cattle, and a milk round. In the first edition of this book I said that Mr. Reed was Brook's milk rounds-man. This was incorrect, even the spelling of his name for which I apologise, and Carole Versey put me right in a letter about her paternal grandfather Herbert Read: "Herbert lived at 1 Elm Terrace, Trinity Road, Mistley, from 1935 until his death in 1962, right next to the St. Michael's school playground, that in turn next to Jack Smith, the Trinity Farm stockman's house. However, despite this proximity, grandfather was not the milk roundsman for Trinity Farm. The house in Elm Terrace was provided for my grandparents as a tied house by Mr. H. M. Poole of Dale Hall Farm in Lawford as he was grandfather's employer. Herbert delivered milk in the Mistley, Manningtree, and Lawford area for Dale Hall seven days a week by pony and milk float, upon which he transported the milk in a large, fixed, churn. On arriving at customers' houses he would carry to their door his half and full pint measures to serve them. Grandfather was one of two men delivering milk for Mr. Poole, the other being Mr. Frank Head".

Carole Versey goes on to say that "There was another milk round from Mistley at that time, carried out by Mr. Ted Kerridge taking milk from the dairy of a Mr. Champness whose farm was accessed from Green Lane, Mistley".

Trinity Farm is remembered today by Trinity Farm Court, and on the other side of the road Trinity Farm Cottage. Almost opposite Trinity Farm Cottage is the path that goes through to Barnfield, and next to that there is the Trinity Free Church, an independent self-governing organisation which grew out of a small group of local people meeting in their own homes. In 1980 they purchased the present building, which was formerly St. Michael's School, and before that the National School operated by the 'National Society for the Education of the Poor in the Principles of the Established Church'. A stone block on the end wall records that the classroom at that end was added in 1904, but the school is much older, having been built in 1814 for the children of the three parishes of Manningtree, Mistley and Lawford, as Joseph Glass recorded in his inimitable fashion:

Herbert Read and his milk float. Mrs. Versey says it shows him "outside his home in Trinity Road also with my grandmother Elsie Read (looking out of the window) and two of their three sons, Francis on the left and Richard, my father, on the right- my father being the youngest".

It is supported by the church, and nation,
Designed for children of a humble station,
That here are taught to read, and write, and spell,
And learn by memory, all the lessons as well.

123

Next to the school is the old cemetery, now somewhat neglected, but called by Glass in 1855 'the new cemetery':

> And quite contiguous to the school we find,
> The cemetery recently designed;
> And as an eligible piece of ground,
> And more appropriate, could not well be found.
> It wants the gravelled path, and even lawn,
> And fragrant flowers the borders to adorn:
> With numerous shrubs, and blooming rose between,
> And all the various plants of evergreen:
> A place where oft, our townsmen may resort,
> And yield themselves to calm and pensive thought.

Opposite the cemetery is the church car park; Elm Terrace, built in 1897; Elmdale Drive, a quiet little collection of new-ish houses; and a bit further along a couple of older residences. On the other side there are bungalows on higher ground, and Trinity Close - another quiet cul-de-sac. Trinity Road continues - past the entrance to the allotments on the right - to the crossroads – with New Road to the left; then at an angle the unmade-up road called Green Lane that went to Mistley

Looking up Brook Street, which still has in part the old blue brick-shaped stones by the side of the road which carried away rain and water borne refuse.

124

Hall past the small Lodge; then what we call the Clacton Road straight ahead; and Long Road to the right. The crossroads was, in the time of Joseph Glass, slightly different:

> Those several roads diverge, on every hand,
> As we before the well known lodges stand.
> Now, on the Bromley road, and near at hand,
> A little way-side Inn, was wont to stand,
> 'Twas named the Cups, and parties here would meet,
> To enjoy the pleasures of this calm retreat.

Going down Brook Street, noticing the view of the distant river Stour, we pass attractive houses and cottages, with Railway Street on the left - which runs up to the railway line and there ends. Continuing down Brook Street on the left is another former shop, No. 16, which once housed the watch and clock business of Mr. H.S. Heath, who specialised in repairing antique and grandfather clocks. His hobby was going fishing in his blue-painted motorboat on the Stour.

Next The Swan public house, turned in 2011 into the Nirala Tandoori Restaurant and Bar, and then the entrance to Mill Lane on the left. On the way along Mill Lane we find a

Members of the Salvation Army playing outside the Co-op store one December Saturday morning in 2007.

Mill Hill in former times, with the railway on the left. The waterworks has yet to be built on the right, so the photograph is before 1908.

number of new houses, some replacing the Salvation Army Citadel which closed in 2002. Built in 1884, the Citadel was demolished because of the high cost of repairs due for this ageing building.

Further up on the left stands the old Territorial Drill Hall where the Manningtree Detachment of the Essex Army Cadet Force meet under Detachment Commander SI Ben Simmons. The 12-18 year-old cadets gain a wide range of skills and experiences, including rifle drill and fieldcraft. The building, which is owned by the Essex Army Cadet Force, is also used by No. 1334 (Manningtree) Squadron of the Air Training Corps on Mondays and Wednesdays. Under the command of Flight Lieutenant Janet Brown, boys and girls of 13 and upwards learn drill, first aid, communications, orienteering etc., and take part in the Duke of Edinburgh's Award Scheme, as well as preparing for flying and gliding lessons.

Mill Lane goes under the railway bridge, and comes out in Lawford opposite the Tendring Hundred Water Services buildings. The water company is now owned and run by Veolia Water East Ltd. The original building has a panel bearing the name of the Tendring Hundred Water Works Company and the date 1908 in the brickwork. The waterworks complex is on the site of a one-time watermill – hence Mill Lane. The mill-pond, formed by damming the stream to provide a head of water for the mill, is still in existence. As local people know, there are many springs in the Manningtree and Mistley area, so finding water has never been a problem. The original boreholes at this site are only used in emergencies now, for our water comes from other boreholes in the area, but all the same it is good wholesome water from local sources.

If we go back down to the corner of Brook Street and Mill Lane we see a stone block in the wall stating that the boundary was a few feet to the left. 'Lawford Parish F.B Capon 1871' on one side and 'Manningtree Parish' are separated on this stone by a line indicating where the boundary was at one time. Capon was a local name, for Robert Capon was a carpenter in Back Lane, as this part of Brook Street was once known. Underneath these stones is a plate stating that the original boundary was 10.5 metres to the west of where the stone is now; it was in the wall of a cottage that has been demolished. The stone is just a relic of an earlier boundary; today the boundary of the town of Manningtree lies some distance to the west, as we have seen.

Continuing down Brook Street, there is a vegetable shop on the right, Stour Fruiterers, close to the corner with Stour Street. Opposite is an open space, where on Fridays and Saturdays Manningtree Market is held. Here is an ornamental pond complete with goldfish and a fountain, and close by the public toilets.

By the bus stop is the Manningtree town sign, designed by Jon Wainwright, which depicts a fishing smack of about 1820. It was made by Paul Gallifant and Arthur Woollard together with pupils at Manningtree School, and was presented to the town in 1984 by the Manningtree and District Co-op Women's Guild.

From the market we travel along Stour Street, a quiet lane now, but not if the planners had had their way. In 1970 the *Manningtree Study And Proposals* plan suggested that Stour Street be widened to take traffic straight through to The Walls; closing part of South Street; closing that part of Stour Street

Stour Street from the market end, with Scoffers Sandwich Bar on the left and Wilf Sadler's Shoe Repair shop on the right.

that bends round to the north to meet the High Street opposite The Crown; and closing the east end of the High Street. The new road would have meant demolishing some houses and requisitioning some gardens, allowing the road to take through traffic along Stour Street, on behind Alma Square, and then bending round to come out by The Walls roughly where The Foreman's House now is.

The idea was to relieve the High Street of vehicles: "The improvement and widening of Stour Street for use as a local traffic road to take the place of the High Street, and to give access to car parks and service yards". It never happened.

Let us now resume our journey along Stour Street as it is today from the Market end. First a refurbished shop which is Sadler's Shoe Repairs. 'Keys cut, Watch Straps, Footwear, Batteries' says the sign above the door stating that it was established in 1939. Wilf and his son Steve, and nephew Philip Lucas, can tackle anything, as they not only have the know-how, but also the old equipment necessary for shoe and leather work still in working order; and people come from miles around to visit these craftsmen.

Wilf Sadler started young in the shoe repair business, for his father had a shop in Market Cross, on the corner of South Street and the High Street. Originally there was a fish and chip shop there, and Mr. Sadler senior rented the premises to live in when he was working at the Brantham factory. However, the owner said that he could only have it if he used it as a shop, so, as he had done a bit of cobbling, he opened up a shoe repair business.

Wilf Sadler took over the business at the age of 20 when his father became ill. He ran the shop until about 1970, when he was told one day to move out at the end of the week, as the building, which was very old, and was built with many huge timbers from broken-up ships, was to be demolished. So Wilf, who was at that time also one of the retained firemen at Manningtree, asked his fellow firemen and others to help fit out an existing building in Stour Street for his new shop. Everyone rallied round to help, and Wilf closed the shop in Market Cross on the Saturday and opened up in the Stour Street premises the following Monday morning. Today, Wilf sells boots and shoes; does key cutting; and repairs all types of footwear, ably assisted by his son and nephew.

Opposite Sadler's is Scoffers, a sandwich bar and a place to buy cakes and bread. Next to this are the wide gates of the Royal Mail Sorting and Delivery Office from where the postmen come out in the early morning on foot, on bicycles, and in vans delivering the mail locally. Today twenty staff deal with an average of 15,000 items every day and take to over 6,000 delivery points in the area.

The four houses set back on the south side of Stour Street are called Alston Villas, after the brewing family who owned and ran the brewery which once stood on the Post Office site opposite.

Reaching the crossroads with South Street, we carry on along Stour Street. Past CMS Carpets providing flooring services; the back of the Tesco store; and on the right, David Darton's furniture restoration business. David has been restoring antique and modern classic furniture since the

Stour Street in 1976 looking across South Street. The business on the other side was the Harwich Radio and Cycle Supplies shop, where they also dealt with 'colour or black and white TV sales and service'.

mid-seventies. 'All aspects of restoration are undertaken including cane and rush seating, desk leathers, upholstery, turning, carving, and polishing' says his publicity material.

Then St. Michael's Court, a small cluster of houses built in the 1980s on the site of a derelict orchard. Stour Street is also the home of The Grand Theatre of Lemmings, an internationally known innovative street theatre group run by David Rose and Mandy Taylor. Formed in 1984, David and Mandy have performed its pioneering street theatre and comedy all over the world. The Stour Street entrance is actually the back door to their premises, and it is not unusual to see them loading up their van with props – furry animals, a pair of stilts, or a giant cannon – into the Lemming's van.

A bit further along is a long low wall – all that is left to remind us that here, behind this wall, was the graveyard at the back of Manningtree Church. For many years, after the church was demolished, this was an open space, with the gravestones propped up against the back wall. As already mentioned, these were moved to the graveyard in Trinity Road.

The building on the other side of Stour Street is where Martin Huggett has his conservation business, specialising in the restoration and manufacture of antiques, furniture, early keyboard instruments, and many other works of art. This building was the home of Manningtree Library in the 1970s, and before that the local Parish Hall. The road then comes to a bend as it curves round to meet the High Street by the Crown. Now we are not far from the sea – that is when the tide is in.

It may seem that the tide is always out, with nothing but a space of mud with boats lying dormant at all angles. But twice a day the tide begins to fill the channels, which gives boaters enough depth for about two hours of sailing time either side of high water. The high 'spring' tides which occur around each new and full moon, rush in slightly earlier and quicker than the 'neaps' – those tides which gently flow reluctantly in at Manningtree in the mornings and evenings.

Before 1970 the high spring tides used to come over the low sand bank and flood into Quay Street, but now the strong

Manningtree beach during the annual Beach Bash in 2011.

Above opposite: Manningtree Fire Station, built in the 1950s, here open for visitors on 20th August 2011.

Below opposite: A call out in December 2010. The Dennis Sabra Rescue Pump leaves with a crew of six. Manningtree Fire Station is No. 17 in the East Division.

sea wall keeps out all high tides and sudden surges, so that houses and the fire station are protected. The Stour Sailing Club boat compound is isolated by big steel doors that are closed when high tides are predicted.

In Quay Street is the Stour Sailing Club headquarters, with very useful clock and tide information displayed outside. Many of the old cottages along Quay Street were demolished and new-ish houses erected with views over the estuary. One of these, "Dry Dock", provides Bed and Breakfast – 'We Will Accommodate Your Friends and Relations With Comfortable Beds and Excellent Breakfast'.

Manningtree fire station, built in the 1950s, is a busy one, even though it is manned by retained firemen who have their various jobs that they leave to man their fire tenders when the call comes. There is no siren these days; that stopped in the 1970s, the fireman being informed by electronic pagers.

Quay Street meets the bottom of South Street, where Jewsons Building Supplies yard and shop are situated –

FEBRUARY 1957   **ONE AND NINEPENCE**

How it once looked through the eyes of artist Albert Ribbans, in his drawing of Quay Street published on the front cover of the East Anglian Magazine in 1957.

formerly Taylor and Butler. Facing up South Street, on the right is North Street and Compass Court, composed of houses built in the 1980s on the site of old cottages. On the left is the front entrance to Quay Courtyard, consisting of new houses on the site of the offices and sawmill of Taylor and Butler, a firm which at one time supplied much of the timber used in the building trade in the area.

Taylor and Butler imported timber into Mistley where the firm had quay frontage at the east end. Baltic Wharf, as it was known, was regularly piled high with timber which was transported to the sawmills in Manningtree next to the customers' order office. At one time, before 1907, Taylor and Butler also had a base for storage in Station Road where the Colchester Co-operative Society store originally stood, but now occupied by Nos.1–5 Henley Court. Here were stables for horses and space for logs waiting to be sawn.

Taylor and Butler, 'Timber Importers and General Builders' Merchants', as they termed themselves, was formed out of an earlier timber business called Taylor and Jessup, listed in William White's directory of 1848. The company, in

Taylor and Butler's motor lorry with driver Frank Foy and assistant Ernie Beaumont.

Unloading timber at Taylor and Butler's Baltic Wharf at Mistley Quay.

their advertisements, boasted 'Established in 1830 when the quay at Manningtree enabled lighters and sailing barges to deliver direct to the company's yard'.

Here, at the bottom of South Street, was the quay where it is recorded that in 1540 there was 'a key, crane, and common store house'. Later the Salt Office was situated here. Within living memory there was a basin, or dock as it was known, for small boats, a U-shaped inlet with a slipway that was used by locals, but this was filled in during the late 1950s. A long quay frontage of steel piling eliminated Manningtree Quay, producing one long straight wall topped with concrete. Only a short section has been retained as a quay for recreational public use.

Taylor and Butler was absorbed into William Brown of Ipswich, and then, in the 1980s, the business was taken over by Jewsons, who about 1990 closed the sawmill, rebuilt the wooden timber storage sheds with modern materials, and opened a building supplies shop. Jewsons concentrated everything on the north side of the road next to the estuary, and their premises in Quay Street and South Street were sold, a selection of houses for the elderly being built on the site now named Quay Courtyard.

The Growth of a Village – Mistley 6

Mistley, with its maltings; busy quay; post office; railway station; shops and businesses, almost qualifies as a town, but local people insist that it is a village. In terms of area Mistley is much larger than its neighbour Manningtree, the parish covering 2,122 acres compared with Manningtree's 49 acres of land, tidal water and foreshore. Even in terms of population Mistley is much larger, with something like double the number of people.

Perhaps it is unrealistic to compare the two in this way. William White in his 1848 directory probably takes the right line when he says of Manningtree that "its parish is remarkably small, containing only about 17 acres of land and 1,255 inhabitants; but the town has a western suburb in Lawford parish, and a large and handsome eastern suburb in Mistley parish. ....so that the total population of the town and suburbs is upwards of 3,000". The total population has grown considerably since then, leading to an even greater contrast between the town and the ever-spreading 'suburbs' of Lawford and Mistley.

Mistley High Street in 2011.

137

The odd thing is that in ecclesiastical terms the town of Manningtree was subservient to the parish of Mistley. Until 1840 St. Michael's Church at Manningtree was a chapel of ease to St. Mary's at Mistley, served by a curate under the rector of Mistley. Only in 1840 did St. Michael and All Angels become a parochial church, a distinction it enjoyed for just a little under 100 years.

The Rigby Family

It is likely that the original medieval settlement of Mistley lay more around the old church of St. Mary the Virgin at what we now call Mistley Heath, south-east of the modern village centre which was called Mistley Thorn. The development of Mistley Thorn really began in the 18th century when the Mistley estate came into the hands of the Rigby family following the death of the Earl of Oxford, previous owner of that estate, in 1703.

Edward Rigby was not very interested in the estate, and anyway died eight years afterwards in 1711. His son Richard Rigby (1690-1730) took over, and built Mistley Hall in 1719, and laid plans to demolish the church at Mistley Heath and build a new one in Mistley itself. He had made a fortune by investing in the South Sea Company and selling his shares before the 'bubble' burst.

Unfortunately he never lived to see his new church completed as he died in 1730 at the age of 40, just as work was starting. This new church was of an unusual design, being built of brick with a 'shallow pitched roof, and little ornamentation outside'. Richard's son, another Richard Rigby (1722-1788), a civil servant and politician, continued the work, with the church being completed and consecrated by the Bishop of London in 1735.

This second Richard Rigby had the idea of making Mistley Thorn into a spa town, and all sorts of plans were drawn up, including hot sea water baths in an elaborate building designed by Robert Adam, but it was never built. However the new quay was constructed during 1777, on part of the site of the smaller one built by the first Richard Rigby in 1727. This new quay is basically what is there today.

The villagers must have wondered what was happening, as so much work was going on in Mistley. At the same time the new quay was being constructed, Robert Adam's plans for improving the church, which Rigby wanted, were being carried out. Two domed towers were added together with a new columned porch and other embellishments. The work was completed in 1777.

When Francois de la Rochefoucauld visited Mistley in 1784 he wrote in his diary: "It contains a new church built after the design of Mr. Adam, an architect of the first rank. I have never seen anything more elegant than this building: there are some elements of the Chinese and Turkish in its construction combined with a simple delicacy. The interior is perfectly harmonious and contains no ornament".

Rigby also enlarged Mistley Hall by adding a new wing, and generally improving the building and its facilities. Rochefoucauld had this to say: "The church is a good point from which to get a view of the house. Mr. Rigby's house is built in white brick on the top of a hill. It is one of the most elegant brick buildings that I have seen. To describe every portion of the house would not only be a difficult task for me, having seen it only in passing, but also quite useless. Accordingly I shall condense my account as much as I can.

"The drawing-room and dining-room are magnificent both in size and proportion and also in their furniture. They are equipped with everything that luxury can dictate and money can buy; the pictures, vases and marble bas-reliefs are really worthy of admiration. The two rooms are divided by a number of ante-rooms which are themselves evidence of good taste. The windows along the whole of this side of the house, which is the main front, look out on to a delightful view – the inlet formed by the mouth of the river bounded on both sides by well-cultivated fields, the houses, farms and churches scattered over the countryside, the town of Harwich, visible in the distance".

An engraving of 1832 of Mistley Hall from Hopping Bridge.

When the young French aristocrat Francois de La Rochefoucauld visited Mistley in 1784 he found it "a very small place, fifty houses at most, which are so well built and so spruce that you see at a glance that they all belong to the same owner. Mr. Rigby owns the whole town. . . All the houses except one belong to him, but the owner of this last one would never sell it to him; and, so that strangers don't compare it with the others, he has painted his red, since the others are white".

The French nobleman remarked on the trade of the port, which he said was "created entirely by Mr. Rigby". His tutor and companion, Maximilien de Lazowski, was more precise in his comments, saying that "Newcastle ships bring the coal which is either distributed by cart into Essex or Suffolk or carried on upriver by barge to Sudbury. The whole neighbourhood brings its corn here to be embarked or stored for the London markets and all the coastal ports. There are six ships at the quay – a fine sight".

Rigby's parties at Mistley Hall became famous both for their magnificence and for the eminence of many of the guests. It is said that local people used to assemble near the front of the hall to watch the guests arrive, and that on one wintry occasion Rigby sent his servants to serve punch to the spectators.

For some 75 years the estate was served by members of the Ambrose family as stewards. The first John Ambrose, a lawyer from Colchester, was appointed steward in 1770, and soon afterwards Richard Rigby built East Lodge for him both as a residence and as the estate office. When this first John Ambrose retired, his son, also John, became steward, and he in turn was succeeded by his son, John Thomas Ambrose, who was still steward when the estate was sold up in 1845 on the instructions of Lord Rivers, whose mother Frances had been a Rigby before marrying Horace Beckford, who inherited the title Lord Rivers.

Edward Norman

One of the major purchasers at the sale of the estate was Edward Norman, who had been a tenant of the Rigby family for a good many years. A member of a local family, he was a maltster and coal and corn merchant and head of a business that in the course of the early 19th century attained pre-eminence in the Mistley area. Born in 1775, he was 31 when he built a malting house on land belonging to the Rigby family at the west end of the Walls, close to the Manningtree boundary. He built another a year later, recorded in a stone in Kiln Lane. By 1828 he had eight maltings on the site. He also had a maltings on Mistley Quay.

In 1819 Norman had a large house, Mistley Place, built for himself just to the east of his maltings complex, and there he brought up his family. He was not alone in buying up property in the 1845 sales, for his great friend Thomas Glover Kensit, who was clerk to the Skinners' Company, one of the London livery companies, acquired land in Mistley and Bradfield, and adopted the role of squire, though he seems not to have become a full-time resident of Mistley because his duties with the Skinners' Company kept him in London most of the time.

141

Converted maltings in the Kiln Lane estate. This one was built in 1817.

The long-standing friendship between the Normans and the Kensits was cemented when Thomas Kensit's daughter Janet married Edward Norman's nephew, the Rev. Charles Norman. The couple moved to Mistley, first living in Portishead House and then, after Edward Norman's death in 1862, at Mistley Place. Edward Norman had certainly done a great deal for Mistley, as his memorial on the north wall of Mistley's new church records.

"His whole life was illustrative of those valuable qualities of industry, perseverance and strict integrity which adorn the character of the British merchant. As his possessions increased he was mindful of his increasing responsibility, opening his hand freely to the poor and destitute and providing for the religious training of the young in this parish by the erection and liberal endowment of a school so that generations yet to come will have to bless God for an act of Christian love after the marble which records it may have perished". The marble memorial survives, and so does Mistley Norman

This original plaque has been re-set in a new wall in Kiln Lane saying 'Built By Edw. Norman 1807'.

Church of England Primary School, which moved from School Lane to new premises in 1981.

Charles Norman inherited his uncle's estate and Janet eventually inherited her father's property in the village, thus bringing much of the old Rigby estate into the Norman family. In the 1860s Canon Norman – he had become a canon of St. Alban's by then – gave a piece of land for the building of a new parish church to take the place of the Rigby church, which was suffering badly from dry rot and had to be demolished, leaving only the two towers standing. The foundations of the new church were laid in December, 1868, after a great deal of hard work had been done by the rector, the Rev. Richard Hayne. When completed it was consecrated in January 1870. The font for the new church was given by Mrs. Janet Norman.

Canon Norman became rector in 1883, and two years later spent £1,000 on decorating the interior of the church. He continued as rector until 1910, when his son, the Rev. Thomas Kensit Norman, took his place.

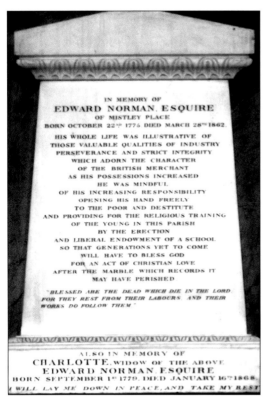

Brooks of Mistley

Left: This memorial to Edward Norman is on the North wall in Mistley church.

Right: Mistley Church from an old postcard.

In his will Edward Norman made a generous bequest to his 'loyal clerk' William Brooks, who also received all the farm and malting utensils. William had clearly begun business on his own even before Norman's death, for by 1859 William had acquired granaries on Mistley Quay, where there were mills and a private rail siding, and in 1863 he set up the company of W. Brooks and Sons. The company, which was in the business of buying and selling grain and agricultural produce, and also farming, expanded in the early 1900s.

An architect's drawing shows the new maltings at the west end of the quay, to be known as Maltings No.9 in Brooks' numbering system, that were built at that time. The plan, by Nottingham architect Richard Hardy and published in *The Brewers Journal* of 15th July, 1901, shows with a degree of artistic licence the quay with lighters unloading sacks of

144

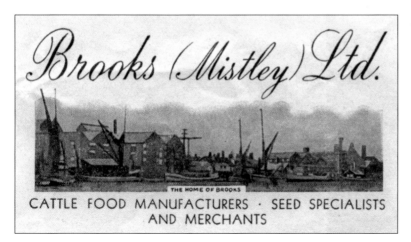

Brooks letter heading of 1952.

grain brought down the canalised River Stour from as far away as Sudbury. Part of Brooks's commercial activity was transferring cargoes from these lighters to seagoing vessels, mostly sailing barges by that time, which took the cargoes to London, bringing back horse manure from the capital's streets for use on land of local farms.

After the 1914-18 war Mr. Hilton Brooks, who had built up the firm in the late 19th century, and Mr. Charles Brooks, began more expansion, with the chief activities being malting; the production of animal feed; and the marketing of fertilisers and agricultural seeds. When Charles Brooks died in 1927 the company reorganised, with many farms being sold off. The company then became known as Brooks (Mistley) Ltd.

Brooks made foods in various forms for cattle, pigs, horses, lambs, chickens, – and dogs. Brooks were pioneers in the 1920s and 30s of dairy cubes, which were made by mixing various ingredients with molasses and pressing the resulting material through a die to make a cube or nut. Brooks were famous for their GB Cow Cubes, made to a recipe of Grosvenor Berry, a farmer from Mount Bures. Another well-known cube was known as the KM, after Keith Miller. In the 1930s cow cubes were sold for £7 per ton. The company won many prizes for cattle fed on GB and KM Cow Cubes.

Brooks had their own pedigree Red Poll herd at Trinity Farm in Trinity Road, where Trinity Farm Court now is.

An artist's impression of Brook's No. 9 malting built on Mistley Quay in 1901 for what was then W. Brooks and Sons. Sacks of grain are being unloaded from Stour lighters in the foreground.

Here there was a dairy producing milk that was sold by milkmen operating a round in the local area.

In the 1920s Attfield Brooks joined the family business, and in the 1930s the company expanded the agricultural seeds division, building new silos on the quay in 1935. Brooks's two sites, at the west end of Mistley Quay and at the Manningtree end of Mistley, employed about 400 people at its height, with many employees coming by bus from as far away as Dovercourt. It is said that 'if an employee's son joined the Boy Scouts and the church choir, he would be offered a job for life'.

The site at the Manningtree end of the Walls, once Edward Norman's maltings and then Brooks's, is now occupied by a housing development off what has been named Kiln Lane. Within this site there were eight maltings with kilns, and between the maltings was a house, Maltings House, which was demolished in 1938.

Flour milling ceased in 1940, after the mill on Thorn Quay had been destroyed by a fire started by incendiary bombs during an air raid. The company continued to expand

A 1929 advertisement.

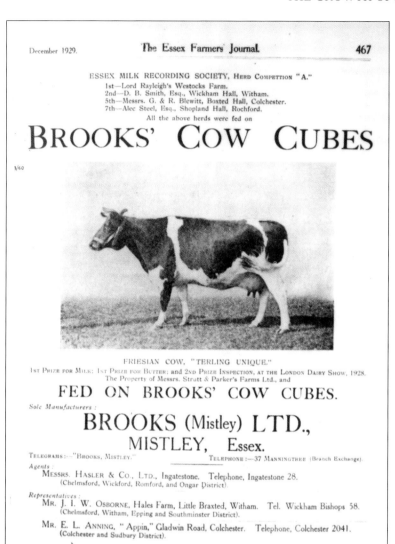

after the war, and in 1946 bought Mistley Place and turned it into a social club and flats. The mill at Thorn Quay was rebuilt when Mr. Victor Crisp was the chairman and managing director. The firm's offices and laboratories, silos, maltings and kilns, and grain drying equipment, were on the main site just outside Manningtree, where there were workshops and a garage and repair shop for the company's 80 vehicles. There were also trial growing plots close to New Road. In 1962 the company was taken over by Rank Hovis McDougall, who in

Loading one of the vessels which plied between Mistley and the Continent in the 1950s. The grain rail-wagon in the background was of the type used to transport Free Rodwell's malt to the Midlands and the North.

1967 closed the maltings and the mills on the quay, and about 1970 demolished Mistley Place.

The derelict buildings on the quay behind Mistley Towers caught fire on 8th April, 1973, not long after Brooks had sold them to a firm of developers who submitted an elaborate plan for 'luxury flats utilising, where possible, the existing old buildings of character on the three-acre site on this part of Mistley Quay, known as Rigby Quay'. The application for constructing these 71 flats and converting the existing building was turned down after considerable opposition to the plans from local people.

Seed processing, grain drying, and storage, continued until Rank Hovis McDougal sold their agricultural companies

148

to Dalgety in 1983, after which only grain drying and storage continued. The office was closed in 1984. Following another fire which destroyed the silos at the main yard in August, 1995, the site was finally closed and sold for housing development. This site now contains new housing encompassing Kiln Lane, The Central Maltings, and Brooks Malting.

The Malting Trade

The Tendring Hundred was a major centre of the malting industry, and Manningtree and Mistley together had the biggest concentration of maltings in the whole county. Although malting had probably been going on in the Mistley and Manningtree area for centuries, it was not until 1728 that the first recorded maltings was built at Mistley by the first Richard Rigby.

William White in his *History, Gazetteer, and Directory of Essex* of 1848 says: "The village of Mistley owes its beauty and importance to the late Rt. Hon. Richard Rigby (the second Rigby), who, in the latter part of the last century, built fifty of the best and handsomest of the original houses, with several granaries, warehouses, a large malting house, and the spacious quay, which forms an extension of the port of Manningtree". White goes on to record that there were two malt kilns in Mistley run by Edward Norman and by Robert Page of Mistley Hall respectively. In Manningtree there was just one set of maltings, belonging to Edward Alston & Daniel Constable Alston, maltsters and brewers.

"Here are also several extensive malting establishments, which pay annually in duty about £50,000", says William White. The 1851 census revealed that 59 of the 331 maltsters in Essex were in the Hundred, and the balance was perhaps tipped still further in favour of the Hundred when, in the 1890s, the big malting buildings on Mistley Quay and in School Lane were built.

In 1893 Robert Free, of London, and William Hunter Rodwell, of Holbrook, together with Robert E. Free and E.N. Heneage, formed Free, Rodwell and Company Ltd. Robert Free

Nos. 5 and 6 maltings were at the east end of the quay, close to the edge. Note the lack of water by the quay at low water.

Herbert Garwood at a sewing machine repairing sacks in the sack store which was off School Lane. He had been with the company for sixty years, and on retirement was presented with a clock.

was an innovator who helped to change malting from a trade employing small malt houses worked by a single man or a handful of men, into an industry producing great quantities of malt in maltings with multiple floors making use of new technologies to improve production methods.

Instead of brick tanks in which to steep (soak) the barley Free introduced large iron steeping tanks from which the wetted barley cascaded on to the malting floor by gravity, and instead of simple fire baskets to heat the kilns he developed new kiln furnaces which were far more efficient in drying the green malt. In a period of about 20 years Free took out half-a-dozen patents for improvements in the making of malt, and he was aided in his work by Offwood Bendall at the Lawford foundry, who built up a considerable reputation as an iron founder with particular experience in the malting industry. The work of the Lawford foundry was to be found in maltings not only at Manningtree and Mistley but at Thorpe-le-Soken and Colchester, and probably elsewhere as well.

Within ten years Free, Rodwell had built seven maltings producing 10,000 tons of malt a year. Each of the separate maltings at Mistley was numbered. Numbers 1 and 2 were on opposite sides of Mistley High Street, Numbers 3, 4, and 7 were in School Lane, and Numbers 5 and 6 were on the quay at the shipyard end.

In the malting process barley from East Anglian farms was taken to the garner floor at the top of the building, where it was dried, cleaned, and stored in bins, then let down by gravity to the cast-iron steeping tanks from which the wetted grain was, after the proper time, taken out and spread on the malting floors to germinate. This way several floors were being used to make malt at the same time, instead of the single floor to be found in the older maltings in use at the time.

The grain, spread evenly about 4-5 inches thick, was turned with malting shovels and 'ploughed' by manual labour to aerate it and ensure that germination proceeded evenly. A careful watch was kept on the temperature to make sure the germination continued at the right pace. Control of temperature was achieved by opening and closing the window shutters, this being crucial to the production of good malt. If it became too warm, moulds were likely to form on the grain. That is the reason why malting was confined to the winter months until the introduction in the mid-20th century of air conditioning.

At just the right moment, after about four days, the 'green' malt was taken from the malting floor and placed in a heated kiln to bring the germination process to an end. This was a very hot and steamy job for the men, who not only spread the malt on the kiln floor, but until the introduction of mechanical kiln turners, had to go into the kiln to turn over the 'green' malt by hand. The kiln floor was of wedge wire, which let the hot air from the furnace below penetrate through the 'green' malt. Dressing and polishing followed, to remove the rootlets which had grown during the germinating period. Finally the malt was sacked and sent to the brewers. The whole process took about nine days to do one batch of about 30 tons. This labour intensive process continued in the seven maltings at Mistley until the mid 1970s.

In 1957 Free, Rodwell and Co. were taken over by Ind Coope, a company with extensive maltings at Burton-on-Trent. In 1969 this company became part of Allied Breweries. This new organisation planned to phase out the labour intensive floor malting system, and on Thursday, May 11th, 1978, opened a new two-and-a-half-million-pound automatic maltings behind Mistley railway station. The new maltings was of a French design, and aimed to turn out 140 ton batches in three to six days, depending on what type of malt is being made.

Today the factory makes wheat and barley malt, and employs sixteen people. The automated plant can run through the night unattended. This is achieved by automation, and combining the germination and kiln processes in one operation.

After several takeovers the present Mistley Maltings became part of Simpsons Malt Ltd. in 2001, and then part of the Crisp Malting Group in 2009. Crisp, who are affiliated to

The malt was regularly turned and 'ploughed' to keep it aerated during its germinating period.

An interior view of one of Free Rodwell's malting floors at Mistley, with the malt being turned by manual labour.

Inside the modern Anglia Maltings, where there is no labour intensive handling in this automated plant that runs around the clock.

EDME through the parent company Anglia Maltings Holdings Ltd, have five other sites, with their headquarters at Great Ryburgh in Norfolk. With the various products, lager malt, distilling malt, wheat malt, and food malt, the Mistley plant now turns out 34,000 metric tons per year. Locally grown wheat is used to make wheat malt for EDME, and barley from East Anglia farms is used to make distilling malt for Scottish whisky; chit malt for roasted malt which is sent to Tivetshall in Norfolk; and lager malt for UK brewing.

Barley and wheat come in by road, and the finished malt goes away by truck also, though there are three or four shipments a year out of Mistley Quay. The steep water goes to an effluent plant to be processed, then is released into the Stour, whereas years ago the steep water went straight into the river, much to the delight of the swans.

When the old floor maltings were closed, some were wholly or partly demolished within a few years, some converted into other uses, and one, No.7, was destroyed by fire in April, 1995.

An industry that nearly came to Manningtree in 1924 was a beet sugar factory; a newspaper announcing that the 'British and Allied Investment Company, whose engineers have made investigations with a view to selecting a suitable site, have found one at Manningtree on the River Stour, where a plentiful supply of water is available'. This was a time when the government was trying to get farmers to grow sugar beet to produce home-grown sugar. Several sugar beet processing factories were built in the region, but the one planned for Manningtree never materialised. Perhaps raising the necessary £300,000 to build the factory, and the initial running costs of £100,000 a year proved too much at the time.

Looking Around 7

Leaving Manningtree and travelling east along the road known as The Walls, running alongside the Stour estuary, we see on the landward side a long low building, now converted into homes, which was once part of Brooks of Mistley and before that part of Edward Norman's industrial undertaking. Brooks was a large firm of more than merely local significance that handled agricultural produce, including grain, seeds and animal feed. The firm had its origins in the middle of the 19th century, when William Brooks was clerk to Edward Norman.

From the time of the First World War to the beginning of the Second there was a private school close by here in what had originally been Edward Norman's house. Mistley Place Preparatory School was run by Ernest Montague Jackson MA. It was also known as The Tower School, because it was originally housed in the building at Dovercourt now known as the Tower Hotel.

At Mistley Place the school had a gymnasium, a dining hall which was one of the big rooms of the house with a

Looking towards Mistley, with Brooks old maltings on the right, which were converted by the company into offices, and later, when sold, into dwellings. This photograph was taken in the 1950s.

fireplace, and teaching rooms. The estate consisted of what we know today as Mistley Place Park, with gardens and the big open space that was used for cricket and football, and for sports days when parents attended. There was an ornamental garden, a well stocked kitchen garden, and the lake by Hopping Bridge. Here was kept a small rowing boat, moored beside the neat path that ran round the waters edge.

The year of 1940 turned out to be a momentous one, as the school magazine, printed in January 1941, recounts:

> Most readers of this magazine will already know that after the invasion of Holland and Belgium the School moved from Mistley Place to Rowton Castle on the Welsh border seven miles west of Shrewsbury. The great move took place on Monday, June 3rd. Two of Beeston's buses, well-known to many generations of teams, and an enormous lorry were drawn up in the drive, together with a fleet of cars which had brought back to the buses those boys who had received week-end hospitality from nearby parents. By 8.30am the

cavalcade had started – a car, two buses, complete with boys and sisters of boys, staff and maids, dogs, baggage and food for the party, and last, but certainly not least, the lorry laden sky-high with beds and mattresses, tables and crockery, cricket nets and trunks, brooms and coal-scuttles. At 6pm we arrived, covering a distance of 220 miles without signposts in 9½ hours. Congratulations Mr. Beeston.

As a result of the move the usual activities of the summer term were somewhat curtailed. Tennis and cricket of the village green type were available, but we had no bathing or sports, though a few races were run, and the bicycle sports were got up as usual by the prefects.

And now that Rowton Castle has been sold to the London School for the Blind, we have to move again, and this time we are joining up with Orwell Park, who in June moved to Honiton, Devonshire, but finally landed up at Bedstone Court, about thirty miles from Rowton Castle. This well known Preparatory School, for many years at Aldeburgh, and known as Aldeburgh Lodge, moved to Orwell Park, Ipswich, in 1937, and many old boys will remember the matches we used to play against them there.

Also in the magazine is the poignant sentence 'A great shock to the School this summer was the news, received in June, that Graham Jackson was reported missing in Norway'. Graham Jackson was Ernest Jackson's son. There is in Mistley Church a memorial to 23 old boys of Mistley Place School who died in the Second World War including Graham Jackson. He was killed on active service near Bodo in Northern Norway in June 1940.

There is also a memorial to Surgeon-Lieutenant John Alderton, who was killed while serving in HMS *Amethyst* on the Yangtse River in China in 1949. In the magazine the Head Master mentions that some young people on their summer holiday, including 'John Alderton, who is now occupied with microscopes and dissection at Epsom, when he is not trying

The Gymnasium at Mistley Place School in the 1930s.

hopefully to unravel the manifold knots in his fishing tackle'. The action in which Surgeon-Lieutenant Alderton lost his life formed the subject of the film *Yangtse Incident*, for which the river sequences were shot on the Orwell in 1957.

The school was never to return to Mistley. The house was occupied by the Army from the summer of 1940 to 1946, and was then taken over by Brooks for flats and as a recreational centre. It was demolished about 1970. The park belonged for a long time to Miss Jackson, daughter of the headmaster. She lived for many years in the house near the church, now part of the animal rescue centre.

Hopping Bridge has an arched brick tunnel underneath, and, at the seaward end, a valve that can be turned to allow the pond behind to be drained. A tide flap stops the sea water entering the pond at high tide. Hopping Bridge itself is hardly noticeable to the passing motorist, but what is seen are the many swans gathered by the roadside waiting for food from visitors who stop and feed them. There have always been swans at Mistley, but they used to congregate off Mistley Quay where they were able to get nourishment from the outfall of water, some of which came from the malting steeps, and with it some bits of barley.

In the 1950s and 60s there were over 600 birds, according to keen naturalist and birdwatcher Ian Rose, who on more

Boys on 'The Cricket Field', now part of Mistley Place Park.

than one occasion counted them. Although a few still hang around the quay area, most swans seek titbits from visitors by Hopping Bridge; so do the rats, and it is quite common to see the rats on the mud by the bank, though when startled they scuttle into holes in the sea wall.

The shore at this part of The Walls was in 1854, according to Mr. Dickens' report, 'very unpleasant at low water. House drains empty themselves on to the beach, and are completely exposed and uncovered for several hours at a time. The surface being broken up into a large number of holes, the sewage refuse is left there to stagnate. The result is, that under almost all conditions, but especially under a hot sun, most offensive and unwholesome smells are produced'.

It was here at 'Mistley Beach' that many local children learnt to swim when in 1931 a swimming pool was built - effectively a low wall around a concrete base forming a large container which filled up with sea water during big tides. Having learnt the rudiments of swimming some then went to Mistley Quay and jumped off the quay or moored barges to swim in the channel.

Standing alone just before the Mistley Towers is Portishead House. Perhaps originally this was where a Mr. Proom lived. Joseph Glass reminds us that Proom "built his hut in a boat, in which he lived with his wife; it was moored

159

Swans near the spot where the swimming pool once was. There are between 200 and 250 swans here.

opposite the end of Mistley Street, and was designated Noah's Ark. After a time he staked it round, to prevent the encroachments of the tide, and planted elder trees for shelter, and thus stealthily secured a place and habitation". Whether or not the site was once Mr. Proom's, Portishead House was built by the Rev. Charles Norman, nephew of Edward Norman, who named it after his former parish in Somerset.

Entering Mistley from the west by the estuary, the first thing that catches the visitor's eye is the two towers, the remains of a unique church built as part of the expansion of the village by the Rigby family in the 18th century. The first Richard Rigby arranged for the building of a church that was opened for worship in June, 1735, to replace the ancient St. Mary's at Mistley Heath. The next Richard Rigby wanted a better church to add to the view of his estate, so in the 1770s he employed Robert Adam to redesign it. Adam considerably altered the church, adding two domed towers, the work being finished in 1777.

Richard Rigby died in 1788 and the estate went through many changes over the next 100 years. In 1870 Mistley Towers church, suffering severely from dry rot, was partly dismantled, leaving the two towers isolated in a churchyard, and a new church in New Road was built on land given by the Rev. Charles Norman. The new St. Mary's was consecrated in 1870.

As we head towards the middle of Mistley there are attractive cottages on the left, and on the right are some rather fine houses and the vestiges of former shops. Mistley had a lot of shops in the High Street at one time, including a butcher, a baker, and an ironmonger. A little further and we come to what must surely be the aesthetic centre of Mistley,

Top Left: This advertisement is about 1947.

Top Right: This advertisement appeared in 1975.

Below: Mistley High Street in 1911.

161

All that remains of the brick-surround pond or reservoir in the garden of Abbey House which once supplied water to the 'dipping well' on the other side of the wall, and the Swan Basin.

with the Thorn Inn, the Post Office, and the Mistley Swan in the centre – a huge bowl or basin once filled with constant running water from springs in Upper Mistley. Francois de la Rochefoucauld writing in 1784 talks about the "circular fountain built upon three legs, where you water your horses. The water runs continually and comes out of a swan's mouth". The Swan Basin was part of the spa town that was envisaged by Richard Rigby, with salt and freshwater baths. That spa town was never built.

> The beauteous fountain, too Sir Richard gave,
> That all villagers should water have;
> The swan, that in the centre sits so fair,
> Supplies what seems her graceful form to bear.
> Pure water found – and gives a large supply,
> To all who thirsty are, and faint, and dry;
> And this pure spring no doubt – near Mistley Thorn,
> Will quench the thirst of numbers yet unborn.

At the time of writing, there is only water coming out of the Swan's mouth in the Basin periodically, for the old

The Swan Basin early one September morning in 2011, with the Thorn, the Post Office, and Abbey House in the background.

system of water coming from springs behind California Road has fallen out of use – even though at one time all deeds of dwellings in the area carried the clause that residents must keep the water supply in good working order. This has all been forgotten now, and at the present time the Parish Council has had to use the mains water supply for which they pay when filling the Basin.

When the Swan Basin was built the water naturally overflowed through the grating on the north rim, and coming out through a lion's mouth into the lower semicircular basin, and then drained to the river. Abbey House stands next to the Post Office. This 'freehold family residence' was built about 1851 and when it was for sale by auction in 1906 it was subject to the right of the inhabitants of Mistley 'to use the basin or reservoir of water' that was on the property. Somewhat later the house was owned by EDME, and Mr. King, the engineer to Free Rodwell, lived there. Today the garden is rather smaller than it was in 1906 when it was noted that it possessed 'fine specimens of Acacia, Lime and Fir Tree'. The house is now used as accommodation and offices for EDME.

Andy Birch, who jointly runs both Mistley Post Office and the T.S.Cook shop with Post Mistress Frances McMillan - 'For All Your Grocery Supplies, Provisions, Frozen Foods, Pet Supplies, Household Products, etc. Bread, Cakes, Dairy Produce, and Vegetables'.

The Mistley Thorn – a pub, hotel, and restaurant, was originally known as just The Thorn. This inn is reputed to have been built in 1723 on the site of an earlier one. In 1839 it was run by one Isaac Churchyard, but these days, in 2012, it is in the hands of Sherri Singleton, who also runs Lucca restaurant in Manningtree, which she opened in 2008. After years running her own catering business in Los Angeles, Sherri came to England with her British husband David McKay in 1988, and soon fell in love with Mistley and the surrounding area. Sherri also runs the Mistley Kitchen Workshops where people can learn and expand their culinary skills with single day workshops on a range of cuisines – French, Italian, Indian, Thai, etc.

The Post Office is always busy with people calling in, not only for anything to do with stamps, letters and parcels, but for all the other things on offer, 'including mobile phone top-ups, electric and gas, banking services, cash withdrawals, foreign currency, National Lottery, newspapers (delivery Service), greeting cards, confectionery'.

Going down to the quay, we encounter a number of names that this has been called over the years. Everyone seems to call it Mistley Quay, but the main section has been variously known as Thorn Quay, Rigby Quay, Brooks Quay, and even Allen's Quay - Robert Allen was the brick-maker at Sudbury who bought this part of the quay at the 1845 sale.

In the 1970s three organisations owned parts of the quay. Allied Breweries, Brooks, and Taylor and Butler. In 1976 Allied Breweries sold their part to Mistley Quay and Forwarding, a newly set-up company. This firm made a success of their business, and expanded by buying adjacent properties, including that of Brooks. According to a report from Mr. S. T. Cass, General Manager of Mistley Quay and Forwarding Company, and written about 1980, traffic grew "from about 100,000 tonnes to over 250,000 tonnes in 1979. The only facilities with which the new company started were an ex-World War II petrol-engined crane, two old fork lift trucks, 6 men, and a small 200 square metre warehouse.

A motorised barge at Mistley in 1957.

"Until 1976 the largest vessel ever to use Mistley had been one of about 950 tonnes deadweight, but since that time ship-owners have been persuaded that larger vessels can be handled. The growth of the port has been greatly assisted by the current trend of thought among some far-sighted ship-owners who, seeing the gradual shift towards inland waterway transport, have recently built numerous 'low profile coasters' – shallow-draught vessels of up to 1,600 tonnes capable of reaching inland ports both on the continent and in the UK. It is interesting to note that the number of such vessels has increased in the last few years and is still increasing. Despite draught limitations of 3.5metres on Neap tides, and 4.4metres on Springs, Mistley recently berthed its largest vessel ever, the 2,700 tonne *Inge Daniellsen*, disproving predictions from 'old hand' locals that the ship would never make it and would block the channel forever!"

It is interesting to note that in Mr. Cass's report he mentions a Mistley to Rotterdam service, a Mistley to Tangiers service, and amongst others a "Mistley to Channel Islands liner service. However, the major ports with which shippers using Mistley normally trade are Rotterdam, Amsterdam, Dunkirk, Le Treport, Rouen, and Hamburg".

The Quay in 1971, a favourite relaxing walk for locals, always with something interesting to look at.

On the main part of the quay here, used by generations of local people to walk on, look at, fish from etc., are the almost-buried railway lines reminding us of a time when cargoes would be brought in by seagoing ships and transferred to railway trucks for delivery to inland destinations. Chubb Horlock remembered that "coal came from the north; malt, barley, and wheat to and from London in the numerous Thames barges; bricks, flour, and small amounts of other goods were brought down the Stour from Sudbury and other mills on the river, to Mistley for transhipment. With all this trade going on, barges sometimes had to lie three or four abreast, and at times there were 20 barges waiting alongside the quays. To load and unload the various ships that came to Mistley was a group of men who were locally known as 'quay lumpers'. They weren't permanently employed, but worked where there was work to be done. If ships were wind-bound or fog-bound then they had to scrape a living elsewhere. I can remember talking to a man who worked on the quay in 1914. He earned 14 shillings a week and lived at Bradfield. I asked him how he spent his money. So much was put in a small box for various household necessities, and this then left him with sixpence. Tobacco was threepence an ounce then, but this was too much for him, and his sixpence went on six pints of tea a week".

Towards the east, just beyond the bend in the quay, was the original shipbuilding area. Ivan Garwood in his book *Mistley in the Days of the Rigbys* tells us there was a shipyard here run by James Betts in the 1770s. Nelson's temporary flagship the *Amphion* was built on that yard in 1778, as well as other warships for the Royal Navy. Francois de La Rochefoucauld, when visiting here in 1784, notes that "At the end of the harbour there is a small ship-building yard, in which I saw two forty-tonners under construction. The trade of the place is wholly created by Mr. Rigby. It consists of coal and corn imported from other parts of England, and four or five vessels are employed in the work of transport. Though the place is but a small one and just beginning to grow there has been an attempt to engage in smuggling, but the individual

167

Local people gather on Mistley Quay on 1ˢᵗ September 2008 in opposition to the new fence.

concerned was not fortunate: he was caught and hanged and had his possessions confiscated and so forth. Near the port there is a lime-kiln which has been faced with brick and made into the shape of a fort. It gives quite a pleasing effect".

Shipbuilding continued at Mistley, coming to an end sometime around 1870. The industry was not revived until 1919 when F.W. Horlock opened his shipyard downriver of the main quay.

The west end of the quay used to be busy with anglers after dabs and flounders, but that is not allowed now as swans often used to get entangled in discarded fishing line. Anyway, there are precious few fish in the river these days. The quay has been in the news in recent years as the owners put up a fence in 2008 to stop visiting boats and barges tying up, and preventing people getting ashore. It was such a traditional sight, with work-boats, barges, and yachts moored at the quay, and ropes and hawsers that visitors had to step over, which gave Mistley that age-old maritime feel. There are moves now to persuade the owners to change the fence for something more attractive in appearance, in keeping with the 18ᵗʰ century quay, and make it more welcoming for visitors and locals who for over 200 years have used the quay for work and recreational use.

The fence that caused so much controversy, stopping boats tying up and sailors coming ashore.

The east end is often busy, with materials piled high on the quayside. Here are ships, cranes, elevators, lorries, and all the paraphernalia of a working wharf, which is a delight to see in these days of shrinking ports and large container terminals. Ronald Reason is the operations manager here, and he oversees the loading and unloading of over thirty large ships brought by pilot up the Stour a year (though the number does vary from year to year), as well as others that do not need a pilot. There are about fifteen employees on the quay, with casual labour brought in when required – particularly when there is more than one vessel loading or unloading.

The ships are much bigger than they once were, and no longer can small freighters turn round by the quay. Now ships either come straight in and tie up, and reverse out to Ballast Hill to turn round; or reverse in, so they are facing Harwich ready for the return journey. These large ships for Mistley wait at the Cork anchorage until the tide is suitable. If the vessel is over 50 metres, then a pilot with local knowledge is necessary to negotiate the narrow and shallow channel of the Stour to the Port of Mistley. A ship needs one metre under the keel, so depending on what the ship draws, the tide has

Shipping helps the economy.

Shipping helps the economy.

to be carefully watched, and even when a high spring tide of a particular depth is predicted, the weather conditions have to be taken into account to make sure there is enough water. At Mistley Quay, when the tide recedes, the ships sit on the bottom in about a metre or two of water.

Ships on the short sea trade routes come and go from Holland, Spain, and other European ports carrying such cargos as aggregates, fertilisers, bricks, broken bricks (for road surfacing), broken glass (for the road building industry),

Bricks from the Netherlands.

scrap metal, poultry ash, and even poultry manure. Some of these materials are loose and are handled by crane grabs, while others are bagged.

The port is owned and run by TW Logistics Ltd., who advertise that they can deal with bulk products such as grain, industrial minerals, granite, metals, and pallet cargos. The company handle, store, package, and distribute materials, and the forwarding part of the business involves containers being brought to Mistley by road from Felixstowe, the contents unloaded and stored, then despatched to their new destination by road. The empty containers are taken back to Felixstowe.

Near the Swan Basin stands Mistley Quay Workshops and café. In this building is a group of crafts-people quietly working away. Next to the café is Grace Wallis, a glass artist and designer, who, using natural forms as inspiration, makes stained glass artefacts to suit all tastes and styles using traditional lead panels, as well as the latest techniques in fused glass.

With a wonderful view of the river, is Con Rendell, maker and repairer of violins, cellos, guitars and the like. Working in his small room, as he has done since 1984, often the sound of a lute or mandolin wafts from his workshop. Next to him is Cooper's Gallery run by Liz Cooper, showing work by local artists and designers; and downstairs, hidden away is Niall Craig, a woodworker designing and making fine furniture. It is not a full time job for Niall, as he is a maths

Top Left: The working part of Mistley Quay on October 25th 2011.The Musca, a bunkering vessel supplying oil to ships, is moored here while receiving maintenance; the Swan Diana, a self discharging bulk carrier, is on lay-by berth; RMS Riga is discharging a cargo of bricks from the Netherlands; and the furthest vessel, the Falcon, is loading grain for Scotland to make whisky.

Top Right: Ronald Reason is the Operations Manager at Mistley Quay.

171

Con Rendell at work in his small but full workshop.

teacher in London, but for two or three days a week he works in his studio with walnut, maple, ash, and oak, bringing out the grain to produce tactile pieces of useful furniture.

Next door to him is Ian Tucker, who makes harpsichords, reproducing the craftsmanship and sounds of the 17th and 18th centuries. These are not just replicas, but instruments made in the same way that they would have been over 300 years ago, and reproducing the exact tonal characteristics of the originals. Ian has been making and restoring musical instruments since 1976. Using a variety of traditional woods; holly, wild cherry, lime, black poplar, oak, beech, walnut, pear, spruce and Italian cypress, together with hand-made hinges and mouldings and historically correct stringing, and decorated with hand-made acid-free paper with designs from his own woodblocks, Ian makes harpsichords, spinets, virginals and clavichords that find homes all over the world. Traffic rushes past on the main road, and the activities of Mistley Quay and Forwarding carry on noisily on the other side, and no one would realise the intricate and exacting work going on in a former dusty grain and sack store.

*Richard and Esther
Brunning in Mistley
Quay café.*

Upstairs the Mistley Quay café is run by Richard and Esther Brunning. Here you can have breakfast, morning coffee, a full lunch, or a cup of tea in the afternoon, while looking out over the estuary. 'Freshly Prepared Food, All Sourced Locally' says their advertisement, with 'Outside Catering Also Available For Weddings, Funerals, and Birthdays'.

On the other side of the High Street there is a road to the south called The Green. This leads to a delightfully quiet part of Mistley, with a collection of houses, including the old Custom House, and a picturesque row of twelve terraced cottages built by the Rigby family. They face 'the Village Green, commonly called Mistley Green', as a parish council notice by the old pump describes the place. This notice sets out the things you cannot do on The Green, such as 'beat, shake, sweep, brush, or cleanse any carpet, druggit, rug or mat, or any other fabric containing dust or mat'. The bylaws also state that you cannot play football, hockey, cricket or golf, and that you must not 'spread or deposit any linen or fabric for the purpose of drying or bleaching'.

Bylaws on the wall by Mistley Green.

Bagging malt at EDME in 1960.

In spite of their lives being so restricted the residents seem to enjoy living in this pleasant setting. '. . .and a person shall not on any part of the Green wilfully obstruct, disturb, interrupt, or annoy any other person, or use any indecent or obscene language to the annoyance of any person'.

The Green was the temporary home of the annual fair that used to come to Mistley during the month of August. In 1907 one tent was showing 'Talking and Animated Pictures' – early sound films.

There are two walkways that leave The Green which make interesting walks. One is named Eileen Jackson Path, after the daughter of schoolmaster Ernest Montague Jackson of Mistley Place Park, which meanders through fields of horses and cattle to the church in New Road, while the other path escapes to the south-east. Here nettles lean in a bit, but there is a way through to a point where you can either go left, through a gate and out through the EDME factory into the High Street, following the yellow marks on the tarmac and dodging the fork lift trucks and lorries; or you can go to the right, over a stream and under the railway line to a field of cows and cowpats. This is Tunnel Meadow. The stream is the one that finds its way out to the estuary at Hopping Bridge.

Back to the High Street, and we start up Mistley Hill. Here on the left is the old No. 1 Maltings of 1896 now converted into 46 apartments by Gladedale Homes. The conversion of these buildings for residential use received much publicity a few years ago when the Prince of Wales took a particular interest in the project and came twice to inspect the work – in 1997 and again in 2005.

On the right as we go up the hill is the EDME works. EDME stands for English Diastatic Malt Extract, a company with its origins going back to 1881, when three people started a business making and selling malt extract. They were Robert Free, he who was involved with the Free Rodwell maltings, together with Richard Southby and Thomas Amey, all of whom had connections with the brewing and malting trades. In 1884 the business officially became the English Diastatic

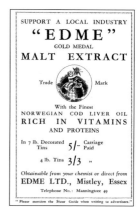

EDME advertisement of the 1930s.

Malt Extract Company, with works on the present site between Mistley High Street and the railway line.

In those days there were many maltings in East Anglia, most supplying local breweries, but EDME, as the firms title became in 1897, served the big London breweries with malt and malt extract. Situated close to the railway line, and not far from the quay, the company had its own sidings and good shipping possibilities. There was plenty of good quality water

*One of EDME's
warehouses.*

176

available (there was a waterworks at one time on the site of the EDME factory, where a huge steam pump lifted the water from the ground), essential for malting, and a place for the used water to go – the river. The company used a lot of water then, 24,000 gallons a day.

To make malt extract the barley is crushed and mixed with water. At the evaporation stage, which changes the weak liquid extracted from the malt to thick syrup, much water is needed for steam and for condensing. At first the water came from the Tendring Water Company, but their supply proved inadequate, and at one time emergency arrangements had to be made with the railway company to take water from their brook on the site boundary. In 1902 EDME sank their own well, making available a plentiful supply of good quality water.

In 1910 things were going sufficiently well for new equipment – a grain dryer, a copper pan and air compressor - to be installed, and a new building for the press room which was built by local builder Harry Rose. By the 1920s EDME was making 80 tons of malt extract per week, and trade with the brewers was flourishing. At the height of the business more than 100 people were employed in malting and producing malt and liquid extracts and yeast. Throughout the existence

Mistley Station in 2011. In December 2005 the buildings were described as 'an architectural delight', and were formally listed as Grade 2 by the DCMS.

of the firm, gradual improvements have been made to the site. In 1950 new buildings were put up to accommodate modern malting drums, doing away with much of the hand labour of the older method of floor malting. During the 1960s, however, the sale of malt extract to breweries declined, particularly when Charrington's Brewery, and Watney, Combe, Reid and Company, ceased using malt extract. At one point the factory was put on a four day week.

EDME began making home brewing kits soon after home brewing was legalised in 1963. The 1970s saw more changes at the Mistley site – first with a take-over by F. and G. Smith, part of Anglia Maltings Holdings. New equipment was installed, coal firing gave way to oil-fired burners, doing away with the cumbersome internal railway system that fed coal slowly into the boilers, and the old Brooks's feed mill building on the opposite side of the road was acquired as a warehouse in 1977.

Mr. Cope bought the old garage site next door to the main works and developed it into a petrol and service station. EDME bought it back when Mr. Cope retired and used it as a workshop and offices until 2003, when it was demolished to improve lorry movements in the yard. At one time there was a blacksmith's shop with three forges on this site by the roadside.

By 1985 Thorn Quay, as the old Brook's building on the opposite side of the road was known, was being used for the production of Tom Caxton Home Brew line, which the company had acquired the year before. A tunnel under the road carried cans filled with syrup to the labelling and wrapping area on the EDME site.

In the 1990s new regulations came into effect banning the discharge of steep water and other effluents into the Stour. These had been going on since 1881 (and no doubt a lot earlier in a more haphazard way), not only from EDME, but from other malt businesses as well. The factory was updated in the 1990s, with much of the older equipment replaced, and some new buildings erected. In 1998 EDME ceased producing beer-making kits, and the bulk supply of syrup for the cereal makers came to an end. A year later the company stopped the production of malt extract.

Now, with a change of name to EDME Food Ingredients, and with a staff of 78, the principal output in the 21st century is dry goods for the bakery, cereal, and food industries – malted and unmalted flours; malted wheat flakes and bakery mixes; and ingredients for muesli, cakes, and health foods. It was announced in 2006 that the firm was intending to move to a new site in the Tendring Hundred area for further expansion and that the Mistley factory would be sold, but this never happened, and EDME is still there today.

Alongside the entrance to Mistley Quay flats, visible in a wall well below road level, is a stone block bearing the name J. Howard with the date of 1846. This is James Howard, a member of the same family as the Howards who went to Grimsby in the 1850s. James was a shipbuilder and ship-owner who was the last to build ships near this site. In 1834 he built the *Countess Wilton*, launching her fully rigged, it is said, ready for sea. According to Hervey Benham in his *Once Upon a Tide* the ship sailed to Norway for a cargo of ice the day after the launching, before entering the fruit trade.

One of the Mistley ship-owners, George Randfield Tovell, seems to have been the possessor of a lively mind, for he was the designer of the revolutionary cutter *Margaret*, built at Colchester in 1853. She was certainly an oddity; her long hull had not an inch of sheer, and her mast was set at about half length. But it was her construction that marked her out, for the keel and keelson were in the form of an inverted arch and the frames were segments of a circle, giving the appearance of a barrel cut in half. Nonetheless, she proved a fast ship, making a voyage out to South Africa in 40 days, which according to a story in the *Suffolk Chronicle* of 9th February, 1856, was 'a feat never accomplished by any English ship'. When she entered the fruit trade she made the voyage from Smyrna to London in 56 days, the average of five vessels which sailed

Left: A train coming down to the quay from the spur line in 1957. The tracks became unused in the late 1970s.

Right: A steam train from the quay waiting for another to pass before it can proceed on its journey.

before her and arrived in London after her, being 74 days. Tovell also seems to have designed some of the vessels built at the Mistley shipyard.

Just before we go over the railway bridge, there is an entrance on the left down to the quay. This is known as Batter Pudding Hill, though nobody seems to know why. Anyway, it leads down to Baltic Quay where once there were maltings, but now just storage units for TW Logistics quay operations. The quay was connected to the main railway system by a spur line that ran down a steep incline to where Horlock later built

Mistley Quay in 1977, with railway wagons on the right, and steel plates being unloaded from a coaster.

180

his shipyard, and then back along the quays as far as Brooks buildings just behind the Mistley Towers. From about the late 1850s there had been a loop that left the main line just east of the railway bridge and curved round in an arc to go under the main line, to emerge by the quay. This horse-drawn tramway was abandoned and replaced by the spur line about 25 years later when the cutting became water-logged. The spur line, and some lines on the quay by the malting buildings, was still being used in the 1970s, when wagons were taken down to the quay by diesel shunters.

There was a signal box at Mistley controlling these activities, but this disappeared when the line was electrified in 1987. Mistley Station had extensive sidings on both sides of the road bridge. Lines also ran into the EDME works. Mistley Station buildings were listed in 2005 as of historic interest Grade 2 after being described as 'an architectural delight'. In essence, the station building has hardly changed since it was built in 1854. The Essex Standard carried a supplement on Friday 18th August 1854, reporting that:

> The event so long anticipated by the inhabitants of Harwich – the facility of railway communication with the Metropolis was accomplished on Tuesday, by the opening of the Branch connecting the Town and Port of Harwich with the main line of the Amalgamated Eastern Counties and Eastern Union Company.
>
> The new Branch railway, about 11 miles in length, leaves the trunk line at Manningtree; or rather at Lawford (where the station for that town is situated), passes behind the town in a cutting, which emerges in what remains of Mistley Park; and at the eastern end of the village a neat station of brick is in course of erection. From thence the line skirts the Cliff (leaving Bradfield on the right) to Wrabness; thence through Stour Wood and Copperas Wood, over Ramsey River, and along the shore to Dovercourt and Harwich. Except only in the cuttings, the River Stour is constantly in view, and at high water affords a charming prospect to the traveller.

We go over the railway on a new road bridge which replaced the old one demolished in 1986 when the line was electrified, and find School Lane on the right. Down here is School House on the left, reminding us that the Mistley Norman School was once here. On our right we see the steaming factory of Anglia Maltings Holdings Ltd, built in 1977 to replace the workings of the old maltings on the Quay which we have already mentioned.

During the years 2004-2006 there was considerable development around the old maltings that stood in School Lane. These latterly belonged to Allied Breweries, and one derelict building, Maltings No. 7, was badly damaged by fire in April 1995, and demolished a few years later. This was one of Free Rodwell's maltings built in 1904. Close by was No. 4 which was partly demolished and the remaining section incorporated into the alterations, along with No. 3 facing the school. This imposing Grade 2 Victorian building has been tastefully converted by Swift Developments and renamed The Malt Store. Here there are 52 one and two bedroom apartments, a swimming pool, and a fitness centre. The first residents moved in during 2005. Beside and behind this is Barley Close, a Mersea Homes development of 27 two, three, and four bedroom town houses.

A postcard of Mistley School in School Lane, with Maltings No. 7 in the background.

Next down School Lane is Rosewood Park, a cluster of new houses on the site of Rose Builders yard. At one time they advertised themselves as 'Rose Brothers, builders, contractors, sanitary engineers, painters, and house decorators'. Harry Rose began the firm in 1896 in Alma House, named after a battle on the Alma river in 1854 in the Crimean War, that tall three-storey detached house in the Harwich Road. In 1906 the Shrublands estate came on the market – a five-acre area of pasture land, fruit trees and garden. With premises also

Converting old malting buildings into homes in School Lane.

183

Rosewood Park in 2011. Behind the houses in the far distance were, and still are, the springs which once provided water for the Swan Basin. Now the water is piped away to the brook that falls into the lake in Mistley Place Park at Hopping Bridge.

included, this was what Harry Rose wanted for his expanding business, so he bought the estate, left Alma House, and moved the business into the site in School Lane. One of the company's jobs was building new sewers for the Manningtree and Mistley area. There was also much work revolving around the expanding malting businesses. In 1930 Rose built the tall EDME chimney, an eye-catching landmark in Mistley to this day.

Known as H. L. Rose & Sons, the company continued to trade through the generations of the family. William and Charles Rose continued to develop the business, building and maintaining many homes and commercial properties in the area. The third generations of Roses, Ian and Bill, expanded the business from the 1950s, and now with Steven, the son of Billy Rose, running the company from its new base at Riverside Avenue East, just into Lawford from Manningtree, the company has expanded with building contracts all over East Anglia and Essex. Since 1995 the company has been known as Rose Builders.

School Lane peters out past Parkside and Parkview Villas and becomes a rough track as it meets the lane that runs up to the site of Mistley Hall, a favourite place for dog walkers and pleasant weekend strolls.

Returning to the main road, we have excellent views across the estuary to the Suffolk shore and of the channel at low tide running out to Ballast Hill, a patch of gravel in mid-river, where it turns sharply to begin its course down Ballast Hill Reach to Stutton Point and so on to Wrabness. Near Ballast Hill the boundary between Mistley and Bradfield meets the county boundary, which follows the middle of the channel along Millers Reach, past the quay, along Thorn Reach, round the Hook, along Manningtree Channel, past the quay, under the southern railway bridge to the White Bridge, and then across the marsh to the river at Cattawade.

Opposite Mistley Quay, on the mud, are the remains of the wreck of a sailing barge, the *Bijou,* that caught alight when a stick of incendiary bombs dropped on Brooks cube mill on 3rd July 1940. It was high tide, and the *Bijou,* moored by the quay, caught alight from falling debris. To prevent her sinking and blocking the channel, she was pushed away from the quay and allowed to burn, sinking a couple of hundred yards away on the other side of the channel. The fire caused much damage to the buildings on the Quay, as can be seen in the photograph taken the next day.

During the 1939-1945 war people pulled together in an extraordinary way. In Mistley members of the Women's Institute formed a Civil Defence Volunteer group with a decontamination building (in case of gas attacks) behind the present Church Hall in New Road. Men not called up joined the Mistley AFS (Auxiliary Fire Service) and were given uniforms, ladders, hoses, and a trailer pump, and practised fire fighting and rescue work on the grass by Portishead House, where a temporary tower was built so that escape exercises could be carried out. There was a First Aid Party, and of course the Home Guard, seen in the photograph from Ian Rose, neatly turned out for inspection on the road just by the Adam Towers.

Above: The remains of Brooks cube mill after incendiary bombs set fire to buildings on Mistley Quay on 3rd July 1940. The house in the lower right hand corner is still standing on the quay today, as are the maltings on the left of the picture at the top. These were converted into flats after malting ceased on the quay in the 1970s.
Right: Civil Defence Volunteers at Mistley about 1940.

An exercise by members of the Auxiliary Fire Service.

On Furze Hill in 1940 there was a concentration of troops to man the ack-ack guns which were positioned in the wood. The men lived in a set of wooden huts, which after the war became homes for people, while other huts were moved to become sheds and in some cases, village halls.

Back to our route, on the right as we go up the hill is a short road named Millers Reach, after that part of the river channel below the quay, leading to a small cluster of modern houses built in what was part of the orchard of Seafield House, which once belonged to Free Rodwell who had their offices there. Then we come to Beckford Road and Notley's Corner, so named after a bakery run by Walter Notley, who delivered bread from his basket when on his round. Further down on the left was the Lord Denman public house. This pub, which

A temporary tower by Portishead House was used for the exercise of rescuing people from buildings. The man being lowered is holding an umbrella!

is listed as being there in 1851, is probably named after the Lord Denman who distinguished himself by his defence of the Luddites in 1816; was a member of parliament between 1818 and 1832; was in favour of the extinction of the slave trade; became a Peer in 1834; and was Lord Chief Justice from 1832 to 1850. He was living at Dagenham in the early 1850s, where there is also a pub named after him. He died in 1854. The licensee of the pub in Mistley in 1937 was George Hunneyball.

Next to the Lord Denman at one time was a family butchers run by C. Barrell and later by Thomas Cook. Almost opposite is what must be the smallest named road in Mistley, Rigby Road. It is paved with grass and goes nowhere. California

This is Mistley First Aid Party, with ARP wardens in the picture as well, seen here with a supposed casualty on a stretcher. This set of photographs is from the Ian Rose collection.

Road starts by Denman House as the closed pub is now known. Much of California Road was built for the maltings workers over a period of time, and the name is almost certainly an indication that the first development took place about 1849, the date of the great California gold rush. There is a variety of cottages and terrace houses, some with most intriguing names – Wiltshire Terrace, Paris Villas, Laburnum Cottages, Evedine Cottages, Michaelstow Terrace, Edith, Pax and Rose Cottages (named after the children of Harry Rose) – and a number of

Mistley Home Guard on parade in the High Street close to the Adam Towers. They may have been joined by other units when this photograph was taken.

189

California Road in 2011.

California Road – flags on a house.

names which have a date following - such as Amo Terrace 1902 and Ivy Villas 1908. One is just M.A.B. Villas.

Coming back to the main Harwich Road, on the corner of Beckford Road there used to be a small wooden hut once used as a butcher's shop and later as a vet's. Every pet, whether dog, cat, tortoise or rabbit, was crammed with their owners in the tiny waiting room, listening unintentionally to everything said, everything done, and every screech, howl, and cry, from the poor creature being attended to in the non-sound proofed consulting room behind the thin and ill-fitting partition.

John Graves at work on his allotment overlooking the railway line and the Estuary at Mistley.

Close by is the Old Mill House, reputed to be, according to D. Jennings Smith in his *Manningtree: Study and Proposals* of 1970, the oldest building in Mistley. Once it was the only building in Upper Mistley, and this was the house occupied by the miller working the windmill that belonged to Rigby's estate. *Essex Windmills, Millers, and Millwrights*, Volume 4, by Kenneth Farries states: 'Presumed smock mill. Described (1775) as a Dutch Mill in Mistley. Owned by Rigby'. A certain John Crozier recorded in his diary in August 1775 that beyond the trees that dotted Mistley Park was a 'fine Dutch wind-mill erected by Mr. Rigby'.

As we go up the Harwich Road, with allotments on our left beside the railway line and an excellent view over the salt water estuary to Suffolk, and Shanghai Villa on our right, we come to the Anchor Inn offering an excellent range of 'real' ales and as it says on the board outside 'Accommodation, Bed and Breakfast, and All Day Sunday Lunch'.

Beside this pub is an unmade up lane to the left called Anchor Lane that leads down to the busy yard of Mistley Marine, run by David Foster, who acquired the site in 1992. Here all types of boats may be seen in a state of repair or rest, as well as specially built equipment for dredging, piling, quayside repairs, towing, and any kind of port authority work. This is on the site once occupied by Frederick Horlock, who set up his shipyard business just after the 1914-1918 war. Later it became a ship breaking yard, when Peter Horlock and his wife were there, living in an old lightship moored in the middle of the business. David Foster carries on the tradition of living close to his work, for he has built a house on stilts which overlooks the yard and the estuary.

Returning once more to Harwich Road, on the east side there is a fish and chip shop run since 1980 by Alan and Sue Pittard. There have been several owners here running this type of business since the property was built in 1955. Before that fish and chips were sold on the other side of the road, from a shop that was once a leather and saddler's business run by Mr. Herbert Davey. Back to the east side of the road, we come to

David Foster's Marine Yard and dock in 2011. Here they are removing a rope caught round the propeller.

Atlas Autos with their lines of used cars for sale. This business has been run since 1986 by Garner Benmore. Then we come to the small but busy general store shop T.S. Cook, also known as Cook's Store, run today by Andy Birch.

Thomas Spendley Cook, who at heart was a farmer, grew vegetables and fruit and kept chickens and pigs on land at the back, selling the produce at first from a shed. This was replaced in 1962 with a shop costing £700 that was later expanded. Spendley Cook retired in the mid 1990s, and the shop is now run by the owners of Mistley Post Office.

Spendley Cook came from a Mistley family (James Spendley was a ship chandler in the 1870s and there were Cook farmers at Dickley Hall and Dovehouse Farm). An only child, Spendley Cook was born in a terrace house between the railway bridge and Notley's Corner. His father, Thomas Cook, had ten brothers and five sisters. All the brothers went into either farming or butchery. Thomas Cook had two butcher's shops, one in Mistley in Beckford Road that was at one time Barrell's, and the other in Manningtree. Both had small slaughterhouses at the back, as was common with butchers

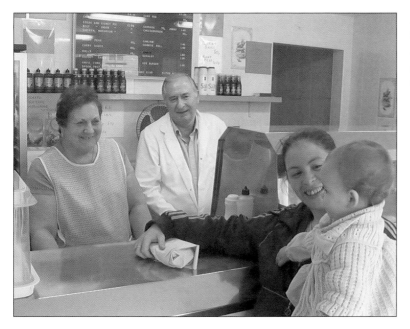

Sue and Alan Pittard inside Mistley Fisheries. Alan has been cooking fish and chips here since 1980.

in those days. Thomas Cook, along with two of his brothers, also ran Home Farm at Mistley, where there was a dairy herd supplying a milk round for the village.

The land at the back of Harwich Road Stores was known as Barn Meadow. Once there were allotments on this land, and nearer the Anchor Inn a gravel pit dug out for building materials as well as ballast for ships leaving Mistley without cargo; the old sailing vessels had to have ballast when sailing light, hence the term 'in ballast'. This is the reason for the sudden drops in land levels. The land was sold in the 1970s when the Stourview estate was built.

On the other side of the road there is a series of 'cuts' – narrow roads leading through to California Road. These are Chapel Cut, with the 1862 Mistley Methodist Church; Kerridge's Cut (Robert Kerridge was a wheelwright and beer house owner in the mid-19th century); and Brunswick House Cut. Brunswick House Cut is named after the large building that was occupied by the 'London County Council Certified Institution for Mental Defectives' as these unfortunate people were termed at the time. Before that, the building was a boy's boarding school run by John Dibley. Before it

*Garner and Spencer
Benmore of Atlas Autos.*

was demolished in the 1980s it was a home for people with learning disabilities. Now Swan Court retirement homes stand on the site.

On the South side of the bend is a round brick building known locally as the Pound. Many villages once had a pound, often circular, to hold straying livestock until retrieved by its owner. Whether this modest building, which first appears on a map in 1850, is really the remains of a pound, no one knows. It had an old stone block incorporated into the brickwork of which the words have long since eroded away. There are plans for a new stone to be put in by the Parish Council.

Off to the right (as we face the Pound) is Shrubland Road, from which there is a road to the left going to Furze Hill, a popular area of woods, playing fields, and amenities, which was bought by the parish council from the Norman Estate in 1957. Mistley Village Hall, Mistley Kids' Club Ltd., and Mistley Rugby Football Club (formed in 1983) are situated here, along with a Recycling Centre for bottles, food tins, and drink cans.

Close by is the 'Secret Bunker' that was open to the public for a number of years in the 1990s. This labyrinth of subterranean rooms was an Anti-Aircraft Operations Centre built in 1951 at a cost of half a million pounds. It was one of four such local control rooms constructed in Essex during the Cold War when the threat of nuclear attack was so much in the government's mind. After being decommissioned in 1993 it remained empty until in 1996 when it was opened as a museum by The Bunker Preservation Trust. Visitors were able to go below ground and see the 7,000 square feet of operations rooms and passage-ways, all filled with authentic equipment telling the story of the Cold War. It closed as a museum in 2002.

Shrubland Road continues as an unmade track down the hill to meet California Road on the right, and further along, School Lane. The track then continues in a straight line to the site of the Rigby's Mistley Hall.

Back on the Harwich Road we come to the fourth shop in Mistley, Tara Traders, once known as Hiskeys and now run by Mr. Raj Patel and his wife Daxa, who took over the shop in 1988. This is a grocery shop, a newsagents, and an off-licence. Almost opposite is the Rigby Avenue and Middlefield Road estate, and further along Harwich Road on the other side Stourview Avenue leads to a number of small roads and closes. At first one thinks that all the road names here are taken from those of local spritsail sailing barges, for we meet Cambria Close, Westmorland Close, Remercie Road and Portlight Close. These certainly are the names of barges, though not all were locally built; the *Cambria*, which was the last sailing barge to carry cargo commercially, under the command of Bob

Left: Middlefield Road in 2011.

Right: Raj Patel outside Tara Traders.

195

Left: Part of Stourview Estate in 2011, looking towards Stourview Avenue with Anchor End cul-de-sac on the left.

Right: This pre-school is run by Deborah Lamb, and is next door to Mistley Norman Church of England Primary School in Remercie Road.

Roberts, was built at Greenhithe in 1906; *Westmoreland* (the barge name had an 'e' in it) was built in 1900; *Remercie* was built at Harwich in 1908; and *Portlight* at Mistley by Horlock in 1925, the last two being part of the F.W. Horlock fleet. The other names are Stourview Close, Seafield Avenue (named after Seafield Bay, an area of the estuary on the Suffolk side opposite Mistley) and Anchor End – at the end.

In Remercie Road stands the Mistley Norman Church of England Primary School, opened in June 1981. The school was established by Edward Norman in 1856 in School Lane and moved to its new premises 125 years later. Now it is run by Mr. Stephen Burnup, the Head teacher. Next door is the Little Lamb's of Mistley Pre-School opened in September 2011. This is the result of hard work and determination of one person, Deborah Lamb. Deborah is a former child minder who is passionate about pre-school child care and helping families. She set about raising the money and getting the organisation going. The result is a purpose built building for twenty six children aged between two and five. The pre-school is open every day of the working week from 8.30- 3.15, and there are also parenting group meetings every few weeks. The idea is to help as much as possible, bringing the community together, so there is somewhere for families to go. The building is light and airy, with toys, games, a creative play area, and small chairs and tables for drawing, painting, and making things – all designed to make it feel like home.

196

Keeping on along Harwich Road, the last house in Mistley is Home Farm. The right-hand turning by the signpost leads to Mistley Heath, on the way to which the road bends round the site of old Mistley church. There is no sign of a church or the graveyard now, the only remaining evidence being stones left from the old church porch which was demolished in 1971. Further along the road we come to Mistley Heath, where there are a few houses and a pub – the Blacksmith's Arms.

Carrying along the Harwich Road, after the speed limit signs, there are the remains of a bridge carrying the road over something. Actually there is nothing there, but once, trains would have travelled under the road on their way to Thorpe-le-Soken – that is, if the scheme for a railway had not collapsed. This was to have been the Mistley, Thorpe, and Walton Railway. The cutting by the bridge has been filled in now, and only the parapet of the bridge is visible to the motorist travelling along the road.

It was in 1862 that the idea was put forward for a line to connect Walton-on-the-Naze with Ipswich by a more direct

An 1851 engraving of the remains of the old church at Mistley Heath.

197

route than that via Colchester. The first idea was that the line would leave Mistley, pass through Bradfield, Wix, Little Bentley, Tendring, Weeley, Beaumont-cum-Moze, Thorpe-le-Soken, Kirby-le-Soken, Great Holland, and Frinton, terminating at Walton. This, according to Thomas Peacock's booklet *The Mistley, Thorpe and Walton Railway*, published in 1946, is what was first proposed. In fact the scheme was considerably altered, and the line was next to have run straight down to join the Clacton line at Weeley.

The new bit of track was to leave the existing Harwich branch line about half a mile east of Mistley station. Work started at Mistley on 6th April, 1864, a cutting being excavated and this brick bridge constructed to carry the road over the railway between Home Farm and the top corner of Jenkins Hill. Then there were disputes, skirmishes and money problems, and work came to a halt. The Mistley, Thorpe and Walton Railway was never completed.

This has brought us beyond the parish boundary, and we must retrace our steps to Mistley Towers in order to explore another part of Mistley.

New Road To The End   8

On the small green in front of the Towers is the Mistley
village sign, for which pupils from Mistley Norman School
contributed ideas. Here also is the memorial which records the
names of sixty Mistleymen who fell during the Great War of
1914-18 and of eleven who died in the 1939-45 war.

   We now go up New Road, called this because it was
constructed when the 'new' church was built. But first the
Church Hall, formerly known as The Institute, meaning a
place of learning, like the Mechanics Institute in Manningtree.
It was built in 1911 at a cost of some £3,000. An appeal for
funds to help finance the building of the hall only raised £300.
Canon Norman stepped in and provided the balance. The
architect was William Douglass Caroe, who specialised in
ecclesiastical buildings.

   The hall is now used extensively by local societies, for
meetings and events, and for video film shows which started

*Mistley Church Hall in
2011 – a hundred years
after it was built.*

199

The interior of the church at a Harvest Festival.

in 2010. These have brought the communities together, with many people filling the hall to watch films, have a drink, and meet friends and neighbours. A few hundred yards further along is the 'new' church itself. This was built in 1869-70, and since 1967 has been dedicated to St. Mary and St. Michael.

Close by the church is the cricket ground with its new practice nets and pavilion extension built by Rose Builders. This was officially opened on 5th August 2011. The Mistley Cricket Club has been in existence since about 1817, and has been on the present site since Victorian times. Next door is the Mistley and Manningtree Bowls Club which has about seventy members, the men competing in the Colchester Borough League and the ladies playing in the Tendring league. This is another organisation with a long history, going back to 1926 when they first had a clubhouse.

Further along is the big open space known as the Welcome Home Field. The land was bought by public subscription as a permanent memorial to all those who fell in the 1939-1945 war, and to welcome home returning servicemen. The Trust was signed on 15th January 1947, and the area opened as a playing field the following year. It has been used for games, special events, and general relaxation, and has a corner of amusements for children to play on. The upkeep comes from a few local donations, but mainly grants from Manningtree and Mistley councils and rents from the bowls and cricket clubs.

Above opposite: Mistley Church in New Road, and part of the field that is now Mistley Place Park.

Below opposite: A photograph by Pamela Browne of Mistley Cricket Club with the new 2011 pavilion extension.

201

There are seventeen trees planted in memory of J. E. Atkinson, H. W. Branch, H. Moss, L. N. Goldspink, R. Sage, N. Sutton, G. M. Jackson, R. Hartgrove, F. G. Lay-Flurrie, T. Osborne, E. Pearson, L. Townes, L. Cook, P. H. Fidgett, M. C. Rist, R. E. Smith, and J. Begg.

The Welcome Home Field was the site of the 1953 coronation celebrations for Mistley and Manningtree, and in 1977 the Queen's Silver Jubilee festivities took place there with float judging, games, music, and a bonfire and fireworks display in the evening. "Lawford, Manningtree, and Mistley Silver Jubilee of Her Majesty Queen Elizabeth the Second. 7th June 1977. A programme of events for the day was drawn up and committees appointed to make the necessary arrangements. These committees have worked with great enthusiasm, and provided the day is fine, it is confidently anticipated that the occasion will be one of the outstanding events of local history".

Below right: The cover of the 1977 Jubilee Programme.

Below left: The celebrations at the Welcome Home Field in 1953. Here is the EDME float going in.

Manningtree, Mistley, and Lawford agreed to "combine with a view to making the celebrations worthy of this great occasion". Actually the festivities began on Saturday June 4th with a fete at Lawford, a tea party for Senior Citizens, and an Open-air Disco. On the Sunday there was a children's tea party, and a presentation of Jubilee mugs at the Allied Breweries Social Club in Mistley. On the Monday there was a pram race, 'topsy-turvy football', tug 'o' war, and cycling events on the

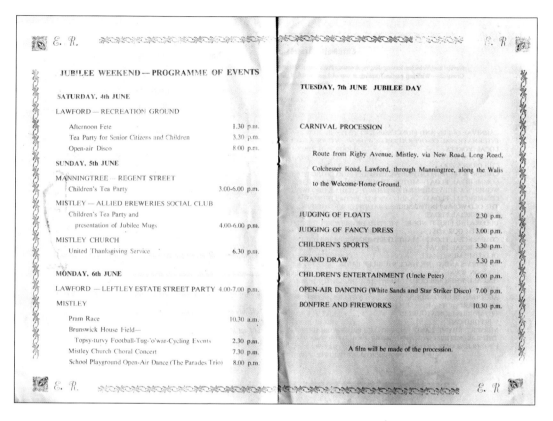

JUBILEE WEEKEND — PROGRAMME OF EVENTS

SATURDAY, 4th JUNE

LAWFORD — RECREATION GROUND

Afternoon Fete	1.30 p.m.
Tea Party for Senior Citizens and Children	3.30 p.m.
Open-air Disco	8.00 p.m.

SUNDAY, 5th JUNE

MANNINGTREE — REGENT STREET

Children's Tea Party	3.00-6.00 p.m.

MISTLEY — ALLIED BREWERIES SOCIAL CLUB

Children's Tea Party and presentation of Jubilee Mugs	4.00-6.00 p.m.

MISTLEY CHURCH

United Thanksgiving Service	6.30 p.m.

MONDAY, 6th JUNE

LAWFORD — LEFTLEY ESTATE STREET PARTY 4.00-7.00 p.m.

MISTLEY

Pram Race	10.30 a.m.
Brunswick House Field—	
Topsy-turvy Football-Tug-'o'war-Cycling Events	2.30 p.m.
Mistley Church Choral Concert	7.30 p.m.
School Playground Open-Air Dance (The Parades Trio)	8.00 p.m.

TUESDAY, 7th JUNE JUBILEE DAY

CARNIVAL PROCESSION

Route from Rigby Avenue, Mistley, via New Road, Long Road, Colchester Road, Lawford, through Manningtree, along the Walls to the Welcome-Home Ground.

JUDGING OF FLOATS	2.30 p.m.
JUDGING OF FANCY DRESS	3.00 p.m.
CHILDREN'S SPORTS	3.30 p.m.
GRAND DRAW	5.30 p.m.
CHILDREN'S ENTERTAINMENT (Uncle Peter)	6.00 p.m.
OPEN-AIR DANCING (White Sands and Star Striker Disco)	7.00 p.m.
BONFIRE AND FIREWORKS	10.30 p.m.

A film will be made of the procession.

Brunswick House field, and an open-air dance in the evening. Tuesday 7th June was the carnival day with over fifty entrants of floats and walking organisations.

On the other side of the road is Mistley Place Park, a 25 acre animal sanctuary which attracts over 30,000 visitors a year. More than 2,000 rescued birds and animals enjoy a free life here in natural surroundings. Here are a variety of creatures - from ducks to donkeys, from owls to fowls. The joint owners of Mistley Place Park are Maureen and Mike Taylor and brother Peter Taylor and his wife Sue. They came here in 1989, later adding a café to the site. Mistley Place Park attracts visitors who can wander amongst the animals giving it that farmyard feel, which makes this a popular place for children and adults.

A bit further along New Road, opposite the far end of the Welcome Home Field is Erskine Road, a 1990s development

The 1977 Jubilee programme.

Charlotte Cleveland is an illustrator who also works with rescued animals. Here she is with Colin the goat. Behind is Clive, not so interested. Both were destined to become meat products at one time, now they lead an idyllic life.

of new houses on part of the old Brooks site. Dr. Robert Erskine was one of the Manningtree doctors in the 1950s, and lived in the High Street at No. 46, with a waiting room and surgery next door.

On land that Brooks used for seed testing, and let out for allotments, a new estate was built in the 1980s down Malthouse Road, where one finds the modern Rectory, home of the Rev. Christine Hills, who is vicar of St. Mary and St. Michael, Mistley,

Mike and Maureen Taylor of Mistley Place Park.

New Barratt houses in Malthouse Road in the early 1980s.

and St. Lawrence, Bradfield. The old rectory was situated in Manningtree High Street, and is now a café at No. 47.

As we go up New Road towards the railway bridge, Norman Road is on the right, named after Edward Norman. On the corner is the unusual Beech House, with a Latin inscription in the wall, meaning something like 'Unless the Lord build the house, they labour in vain that build it'. This was the Masonic Lodge building put up in 1873, which accounts for the rather unusual design.

Further along Norman Road is where the premises of C. Stone and Son, coal and coke merchants, once was. Stones delivered to houses and businesses in the area, originally by horse and cart, and later by a couple of Morris commercial lorries, one of c.1935, and one of c.1952.

Towards the end of the 19th century Charles Stone built a pair of semi-detached houses in Norman Road next to the yard. One was for himself, named *Coalville,* the other for his son. Semi-detached houses are normally identical, but if you look closely at this pair, the house on the left is slightly smaller than its neighbour. Charles Stone's *Coalville* had a purpose built bathroom, said to be the first such bathroom in the area. The house for his son was called *Brooklyn,* and did not have a bathroom.

He had to wash using a tin bath in the kitchen. The porch is slightly narrower than that of *Coalville*, and the windows are closer together.

The Essex writer Hervey Benham, who went to sea in barges during time off from editing the *Essex County Standard*, records in *Down Tops'l* that Charles Stone was one of eight brothers, all of who were involved with barges either as owners or skippers – or both. Harry Stone, who lived round the corner in Cumberland House in Oxford Road, had the big boomie barge *Genesta*, which he kept up like a yacht; Jim Stone had the boomies *Harold* and *Eliza H*; and Charles Stone had the spritty *Centaur* built for him at Harwich in 1895.

When John Wood took over the business in 1973, the bags of coal were still filled, weighed, and loaded onto lorries by manual labour. In 1974 C. Catling & Son's coal business at Bradfield was taken over, and the two businesses were run as C. Stone & Son from the yards in Norman Road and Kings Street in Bradfield. In 1985 C. Stone and Son was itself taken over by D. Humphrey & Sons in Artillery Street in Colchester.

Looking along Norman Road, with Mr. Gary Donoghue leaning on the gate of Beech House.

Opposite the entrance to Norman Road, there is a row of cottages called Reform Terrace which were sold at auction in 1906. The catalogue information about these eight houses is interesting: 'Each Tenement contains two up and two downstairs rooms, with pantry under the stairs. Outside: wash-house with sink and WC, and the Tendring Hundred Water is laid on'. The tenants at the time were: No. 1, J. Denton; No. 2, Mrs. Silburne; No. 3, Mrs. Ford; No. 4, Mrs. Yell; No.5, H. Gray; No. 6, J. J. Bloomfield; No. 7, Mrs. Collins; No. 8, W. Cuthbert (Policeman). The rates were between £6 and £9 per year.

Next is a new railway bridge over the branch line to Harwich. This line, built in 1854, had not come without tragedy. During the building of the original bridge, two men were killed. The report in the paper is as follows:

> About 5 o'clock on Wednesday morning a shocking accident occurred at the Railway Bridge erecting on the Harwich Railway, adjoining the Police Station, Mistley, by which two men lost their lives, and two others were much injured. It appears that six men were employed under the arch to remove the centres, which

had been eased the day previous; they had scarcely commenced work, when the whole of the centres, which were very heavy, having a quantity of earth upon them for the purpose of raising the crown of the arch, gave way. Nathan Taylor, aged 28, of Mistley, was killed on the spot; and Thos. May, aged 33, of Bradfield, labourer, survived the accident only an hour and a half; each of them leaving a wife and four children to mourn their loss. They were very steady and industrious men and good husbands. James Mason was very much cut about the head and otherwise seriously injured; and William Clarke received an injury in the back. The other two men, Robert Smith and William Moss, most miraculously, escaped unhurt.

Over the railway bridge, on the left, we come to what is the Mistley Police Station. This was closed to the public at the end of November 2011 as part of Essex Police's plan to save £41million by 2015. There has been a police station building in New Road, Mistley, with cells and a courtroom, since 1853, and when Joseph Glass published his book in 1855, it was still somewhat new.

Mistley Police Station in 2011 just before it closed to the public.

Constructed lately, for a righteous cause,
Where equal justice may enforce the laws;
Also a rendezvous for the police,
Those worthy keepers of our country's peace;
To which they have a place that's well constructed,
Safely to incarcerate the misconducted,-
Those worthless culprits, ever in the wrong,
With bricks and mortar, firm, secure and strong.

Before there was a police station it seems the method of detaining unruly people was to put them in a cage.

For this intent, and in a former age,
Our previous sires possessed a wooden cage,
It stood contiguous to the Lion Inn,
Dingy without, and desolate within.
Between the upright bars, the boys threw stones,
And broken tiles and bottles, bats, and bones;
To thieves and rogues, it was a serious case,
To be consigned to such a wretched place.

In 1960 the courtroom closed, and a year later the station was demolished and replaced with a new style building

The Park in 1907. The building on the left was once the Essex Arms.

consisting of two police houses, which were soon altered to turn it into Mistley Police Station. Now, after closure to the public was announced in 2011, it seems that the building will be retained as a base for police officers looking after the local parishes.

Next – The Park, a loop of close-knit dwellings which include a substantial house with 'Essex Arms' above the door. This was a beer house run by John Wyncoll, a bricklayer, in 1861, when it appears he opened it. Wyncoll is also listed as victualler of the Waggon and Horses in 1866.

The Essex Arms is just a private home these days, but when it was sold in 1888, the conveyance mentioned that it was formerly a beer house in Park Street. The Park began it seems, with 'four labourers cottages' in 1851. Ten years later there were seven houses. The road, which is still not made up, and now known as just The Park, goes round to more houses on the other side, some of which were built later. It comes out on New Road again.

Opposite, on the corner of Oxford Road, was the Waggon and Horses, renamed in 2006 The Wagon. Four years later it closed completely and is now boarded up awaiting some sort of development. Just by this, on the other side of Oxford Road, to the left of Oxford House, is a lane of houses called Barnfield. An old photograph shows two of these – not much changed.

New Road continues past The Chase, a short lane on the right with a passage through to Trinity Road; and then to the crossroads. Here New Road meets Long Road, and the Clacton road meets Trinity Road. Here we come to the end of our tour.

This old picture shows houses in Barnfield, a lane off the top of Oxford Road.

> And now, although we may not further dwell,
> 'Tis evident we're able to foretell,
> Advantages most likely to take place,
> To be enjoyed by a succeeding race.
> And soon when temperance is with triumph crown'd
> And sways the willing hearts of all around;
> Then England shall be rich indeed, and free,
> And all most happy found in Manningtree.

211

Select Bibliography

Benham, Hervey. *Once Upon A Tide*. George Harrap & Co. Ltd. London. 1955

Boyes, John, and Russell, Ronald. *The Canals of Eastern England*.
David and Charles. 1977

Cleveland, David. *Manningtree Station*. David Cleveland, Manningtree. 2008

Fisher, Douglas. *Manningtree, Mistley, and Lawford in Old Postcards*. Netherlands. 1996

Garwood, Ivan. *Mistley In The Days Of The Rigbys*. Lucas Books. 2003

Glass, Joseph. *Reminiscences of Manningtree and Its Vicinity*.
Judd and Glass. London. 1855

Hopkins, Matthew. *The Discovery of Witches, An Answer To Several Queries*.
London. 1647

Horlock, A. H. *Mistleyman's Log, Chronicles Of A Barging Life*.
Fisher Nautical Press. 1977

Horlock, Bob, and Fryer, Mike. *Visiting The Past*. R. J. Horlock, Mistley. 2011

Hughes, Carlyon, *The History of Harwich Harbour*. Dovercourt. 1939

Our Story – The History of Three Parishes. Manningtree Branch WEA. 1954

Peacock, Thomas. *The Mistley, Thorpe, and Walton Railway*. Peacock. 1946

Pictures From The Past of Manningtree, Mistley, and Lawford. Manningtree Museum.

Pictures From The Past of Manningtree, Mistley, and Lawford. Vol 2.
Manningtree Museum.

Rochefoucauld, Francois de la. *A Frenchman In England*. Cambridge
University Press. 1933

Sage, Ivan. *Lawford Life*. IRS. 2002

Smith, D. Jennings. *Manningtree: Study And Proposals*. Essex County Council. 1970

Smith, R. S. *St. Michaels, Highfields, The Wesley School*. 1978

White, William. *History, Gazetteer, and Directory of the County of Essex*. 1848

Kelly's Directories of Essex

Index

E

Eastern Electricity, 113
EDME, 92, 154, 163, 174-179, 184, 202
Eels, 50, 52, 53, 54,
Elite, see Railex
Elmdale Drive, 124
English Terrace, 67
Entire Computers, 96, 98
Erskine Road, 203
Erskine, Dr. Robert Martley, 68, 76, 204

F

Fairhall, John, 61
Farthing's Furniture, 81
Fire Station, 132, 133
Fishing, 49, 50, 51, 52
Fitch, Joshua, 95,
Foster, David, 191, 192
Foundry Court, 95
Free, Rodwell, 149, 150, 151, 152, 163, 187
Fryer, Mike, 8
Furze Hill, 194

G

Gallifant, Paul, 127
Gant, Peter, 71
Garwood, Gemma, 86
Garwood, Herbert, 150
Garwood, Ivan, 7, 167,
Gas Board showroom, 119
Gasfield, 3, 114
Gasworks, 30, 113, 114
Gee, Mr. and Mrs., 76
Glass, Joseph, ix, x-xii, 8, 13, 18, 20, 22-23, 28, 29, 42, 68-69, 73, 83, 89, 111, 115, 119, 122, 124, 162, 209, 211

Grand Theatre of Lemmings, 130
Gwinnell, R., 81, 107

H

Hair @ Number Ten, 92
Harwich Radio and Cycle Supplies, 109
Harwich Road Stores, 193
Harwich Road, 191, 195, 197
Hebblewhite, Martin 86, 87
Hills, Rev. Christine, 204
Hilton Close, 3
Hog Marsh, 20
Home Guard, 185, 189
Honeywood family, 67
Honibal, Thomas, 30
Hopkins, Matthew, 8, 9, 10, 11, 12, 112
Horlock family, 45, 47, 49, 59, 180, 191
Horlock, Bob, 8, 45
Horlock, Chubb, 47, 49
Horlock, F. W., 45, 46, 47, 58, 59, 168, 191, 196
Horsley Cross, 5
Hoskyns, Dr. John, 98
Howard family, 49, 179
Howard, Thomas, 49
Howells, Dennis, 89
Hub, The, 81
Huggett, Martin, 130
Hughes-Stanton, Blair, 66
Hughes-Stanton, Penny, 66

I

Ike@47, 70
Independent Chapel, 112, 113, 118

J

Jackson family, 155-158, 175, 202

Jewsons, 136
Jiggins, Tony, 50, 52

K

Kamanda, Dr. Mary, 98
Kelly, Dr. John, 68
Kenny, Peter, 90
Kensit, Thomas, 141, 142
Kerridge's Cut, 193
Kiln Lane, 3, 68, 141, 142, 143, 146, 149
King's Head, 16, 23, 24

L

Lamb, Deborah, 196
Lane, The, 79, 80, 81
Lawford Iron Works, 95
Leander Cottages, 101
Library, Manningtree, 81, 83, 131
Little Lamb's of Mistley Pre-School, 196
Long Road, 125, 211
Lorberg, Phil, 96, 98
Lord Denman, 26, 27, 28, 187, 188
Lucas family, 28, 61, 128
Lucas, Jack, 50
Lucca Restaurant, 75, 164
Lushington Road, 4, 98, 100

M

M. J. M. Financial Services, 108
Malt Store, The, 182
Malthouse Road, 204, 205
Malting, 149-154, 158
Maltings, 3, 31, 57, 146-154, 175
Manifest Theatre, 3, 116, 118, 119
Manningtree Delicatessen, 81
Manningtree Grill & Pizza, 92
Market Cross, 57, 81, 83, 105
Market, 13, 14, 15, 127